# One of Ten

# One of Ten

Herb Johnson

**To order additional copies of this book, contact:**
Xlibris Corporation
1-888-795-4274
www.Xlibris.com
Orders@Xlibris.com
65944

January 1942

# TABLE OF CONTENTS

# PREFACE

*Eighty years have an advantage. You find that as the years pass, there are many changes in the world around you. I look back over the multiple years and find each one unique. This I decided when I finally gathered up my notes, with the insistence of my son Greg and daughter Barbara, and put them into a story of my life. I have always maintained that every person holds an interesting story of his life and so many pass on without any record. I look back on my parents. I know very little about my father's younger years such as how he spent his youth before he met my mother. I know my mother lived in many places, but I know nothing about them. How I wish I could ask them many questions about their younger lives, friends, schools, relatives, and so much more. We often think of these things when it is too late.*

*It is fairly easy to trace our genealogy through the years, but this does not tell us anything about the little stories that each person has. There are no records of all the phrases, quotations, poems,and myths that the years hold.*

*The following story of my life is not to be a statement of fact, but is life as I remember it. I know my children and grandchildren will enjoy reading it. I wish to thank them and also my wife, Marnie, who encouraged me to go ahead and finish this writing. I also want to thank my cousin, Laurel Grimsted, who took my rough copy and made it into a finished product.*

*Herb Johnson*

# EDITOR'S NOTE

*Herb wrote a delightful autobiography. His positive attitude is reflected in his preface which starts, "Eighty years have an advantage." Herb's love for life and people shows throughout the book. He is candid and down to earth. I am honored to be Herb's editor. Working on this project has been a heart warming experience. It has enriched my relationship with Herb and Marnie. I treasure our sharing of stories and visits. Although the book may be done, I know the sharing will continue. I want to thank Rick, my husband, who volunteered me. I also want to thank Herb who has inspired me to start on my own family stories.*

*Laurel Grimsted*

# CHAPTER 1

## The Early Years

## 1921—1933

It all began on April 21, 1921 on a ranch miles from Re Heights, South Dakota. When the doctor arrived, as told by my mother, I was already present and sucking my thumb. My memories of the following years are few—lost in a corn field and climbing a hay stacker when I was between two and three. I was the fourth of four boys. Howard, the oldest, was the sincere one. Justin, the second, was the one who always did his own thing. George, the third son, was the great fighter and defender. My father, Henry Eddie Johnson, was a native of Oldham, South Dakota. He was the fourth son of J. P. Johnson who was a Dakota pioneer. My mother, Alice Boleta Setbacken, was born in Lake Preston, South Dakota. She was the fifth child of Jens P. Setbacken. Mother was a full Norwegian. Dad was half Swede and half Dane.

In my early years, I had few outstanding qualities. I had large tonsils, crooked teeth and the ability to sunburn in the shade. My first real memories were when we moved to Falkton, South Dakota, where my dad operated a pool hall. In Falkton, my pal was a girl about five years older. She was slightly retarded, but to me she was a real pal. Together we enjoyed the company of a very old man with a long beard. The two of us listened to his many stories while sitting on his back porch. I remember running after the ice wagon and begging for a piece of broken ice. Mom made the best cold drinks. I will never forget walking to meet Dad when he came home from the pool hall. I had to cut across the street so as not to go in front of the Catholic Church because I had heard they had guns in there and would shoot you. Where this story came from, I don't remember.

I was not fortunate to know my grandparents well. Grampa Johnson (J.P.), I don't remember at all. I only know what I heard in later years. He was strict and rather a ruthless man. I was told by Dad that he left home when only 14. He was unable to stay at home because of abuse. Gramma Johnson was quite different. I remember her well, especially sitting on her lap. I always felt so secure. She named me and also gave me a stuffed pig which my daughter, Barb, still has. Gramma Setbacken is only a slight image in my memory. She seemed to be always working and very quiet. Grampa Setbacken had a long white beard and a gruff voice that scared the devil out of me. My favorite uncle, Benny, took me down to the barn one day. When Grampa Setbacken saw me, he said in a rather loud voice, "What is that kid doing down here?"

After a year in Falkton, we moved to the Lars Carlson farm because Dad wanted to get back to farming. This farm was a few miles south of Hedlund, South Dakota. Our closest neighbors were the Sedersoms. They had a boy George's age and a girl the same age as me. With her, came my first enlightenment. We took our clothes off down in the hay barn and found out we were gifted differently. This was getting to be a close examination when her older brother and George arrived.

I have fond memories of the Lars Carlson farm and going to barn dances in the bob sled. I remember how cold it was; but so warm under the old horse blanket. One dance I remember well had an old man playing the fiddle with sweat dropping off the end of his nose. Other recollections include Maxine's mother going to town to buy groceries with a cow being led behind the car, Dad's smoke house with bacon and hams, rhubarb pie, fresh horse radish being ground and how it would bring tears to your eyes, and the visit to our neighbors' to hear the Jack Dempsey fight.

The house on the Lars Carlson farm was very close to a large grove of trees. One of Dad's favorite pastimes was to sneak into the trees when us boys were not watching. The next thing we knew, there was a horrible growling noise and the trees were shaking. I think Howard and Justin were wise to him; but poor George and I would become terrified and run for Mom and the house. Dad loved to box so he bought a set of boxing gloves for us. He would have two of us put on the gloves and hold a broom stick between us and let us go at it. George proved to be the best boxer.

One Sunday, the family went for a picnic at a lake. I was born to fish so when we arrived I asked Dad if we could do so. I will never forget how he hunted along the shore until he came up with a stick, fishing string, and a hook. I found some worms so I was in my glory.

One big event was the day Bob was born. My Aunt Alpha served us four boys chocolate cake. There was one piece left which she set up on the piano. It was plain torture to be unable to reach that cake. Bob, a little red faced baby, was brought into the room squealing his heart out. I wonder if he knew what was in store for him from his older brothers in the years to come.

From the Lars Carlson farm, we moved to Lake Preston in about 1925. Dad had been hired on the rail gang for Northwestern Railroad. We brought with us a milk cow and a baby bull named Duke. We had a neighbor lady, Mrs. Hookie, who was always baking bread. The bread hot out of the oven with butter and sugar was beyond description. Our milk cow produced more milk than our needs so a milk route was put into effect. This was a job for the three older boys. I remember Uncle Alfred, who was big and fat, always stopping by and asking Mom for bread with cream over the top. It was amazing how much he would eat. My favorite time was when Mom would ask me to go to the store for a soup bone or some other item. It would take only a few pennies to get a package of liver. The soup bones were free. Getting into Beck's Grocery store was a real treat with all the cookies in the bins, peanut butter in kegs, pickled herring in barrels and many other mouth watering goodies. One of the hardships of the trips to the store was a sharp dip in the sidewalk that always threw me resulting in skinned knees and bumps.

Lake Preston was not a good place for four boys off the farm. Poor Dad and Mom had their hands full just trying to keep track of us. Brother Justin was always skipping school, and George and I were caught in the Electric Company storage yard removing all the copper and brass we could from the light fixtures and junction boxes. We had a ready market for this at the local junk dealer who did not ask any questions. Shortly after this, Justin, George and I found our way into a recently vacated house. When we went upstairs, we discovered a hole in the floor where the stove pipe vented to the roof chimney. After dropping anything we could find down through to the front room floor, we all took turns in relieving ourselves. We came home to find out we had been reported on by the neighbors. I escaped punishment because I was the smallest one. Things did not improve for Dad. He found out that we three boys had been making daily trips to the railroad yard to put items on the train tracks. Crossed pins made scissors, pennies made real trading items and some of the larger items did not fare well with the trains or the yard crews.

One day our lives changed when a strange man showed up. We found out he was Dad's Uncle Bill. He had come from western South Dakota where he had a farm. He convinced Dad that he should move out there with the family. We were all excited about living on a farm again so we packed everything up. It all had to go—furniture, kids, dog, cow and calf. Dad and three boys (Howard, Justin, and George) drove the model T Ford. Mom, I, Bob, and Charley went by train to Lemmon, South Dakota. The animals and furniture were put into a box car for shipment to our new home. It was my first train ride. What excitement! When you went to the bathroom, you could see the train track going by through the toilet hole. Dad was waiting for us when we arrived in Lemmon. Uncle Bill's farm was about forty miles south. The house was small, but it had an upstairs that Uncle Bill was dividing into bedrooms.

The barn had a great hayloft. It was exciting to have a big creek running right by this barn. Also, we had a school house close by. This was the year I started my education. I immediately fell in love with my teacher. I was the only first grader and had a little table and chair right up by this teacher.

Uncle Bill had a wild dog that stayed with the pigs. He was a problem as he ate all the eggs in the chicken house. Dad decided that the dog had to go. One morning he caught the dog in the chicken house and shot him. We were glad to see the end of this animal as he was very wild and could not be tamed.

This year was to be my first visit to a hospital. My tonsils and adenoids had to come out. What a frightening experience. I remember struggling and screaming as they held me down to administer the ether, and then vomiting up blood after the operation. It took many years to get over this experience.

During the summer months, it was hot. George and I took refuge in the basement. It had dirt walls and floor. We used bottles for cars and an elaborate system of roads and tunnels. Our garages were holes dug in the bank. Our problem was that salamanders would hole up in the garages and we would have to extradite them each day.

Our first Thanksgiving dinner was with the Merrets at their house. They were our closest neighbors. All the children went for a long walk and came back to find the older people had already eaten. We all had to wait outside until they finished their pie and talk. Boy was I hungry. To make it worse, Mr. Merret handed me a dish of bones. After some wait, we finally made it to the table.

Christmas arrived and so did the depression. Dad came home from town with all the milk, cream, and eggs—no buyers. The creamery had closed down. We were without groceries. Thank God for the farm. At least we had eggs, milk, meat, and also the things Mom had canned. I remember Dad telling Mom that we would be going to town at night. He was butchering some of the cattle and selling the meat to the restaurants.

The day before Christmas, Dad and us four older boys took the sled and walked back into the hills to find a Christmas tree. We decorated it with strings of pop corn and cranberries. Mom came up with a few beautiful decorations such as balls and birds that clamped onto the tree, and also candles. There was not much under the tree. We had saved our candy and oranges from the school program so that helped.

A few news stories that I can remember were the Flying Fool Arrives in France, the Democrats Sweep the Nation, and the Talks by our President, Franklin Roosevelt. I was fortunate to see Calvin Coolidge when he was president. He and his wife came through Lake Preston on their way home from the hills. They both came out on the vestibule of the rail car and waved. In all these years, he is the only president I have personally seen.

One day a man in an old car drove into our farm along with a bunch of thin and hungry hounds. He apparently knew Dad, for the two of them left for somewhere. The stranger told us not to turn the hounds loose before he came back. George asked him if they could catch jack rabbits and was assured that would be no problem. Well, the minute Dad and the stranger were out of sight, the hounds were free. We took them down to a pasture that was fenced in. The six or seven of them were chasing rabbits and gulping them down as soon as they caught one. Hair, legs, ears, and all were gone in just one gulp. We had them all tied up and well fed when Dad and the man came back. We may have changed some coyote hounds into rabbit hounds.

Well Mom surprised everyone with the arrival of the first girl. She was to be named Dolores. She was born in the Shade Hill hospital. It was great times for us boys to think we finally had a baby sister.

We soon learned that Uncle Bill was a very strange man. He took joy in spanking Justin for any reason. It became so bad that Mom and Dad decided the only answer was to move. That's when the Joe Moore farm came into our lives. This was only thirty miles away which made the move rather easy. The farm was owned by the county. Taxes I guess. It had a fairly nice house and out buildings.

School was only a half mile away and we had real close neighbors. Here I met my pal and classmate, Clarence Stanley. We shared many good times together. Our greatest pastime was snaring gophers. Clarence, many years later, was to lose his life with the Renault Flying Tigers. He went down in his first dog fight with a Jap.

A real experience arrived. Dad announced he trapped an old female silver badger and that he needed our help to dig out the young pups. Dad and us four boys succeeded in getting the two pups, one male and one female, out. We took them home and made pets out of them. They became as tame as a pair of kittens. Their favorite food was bread soaked in milk. We named them Nip and Tuck.

Later we had another experience with badgers. One day Justin and I were out in the pasture and spotted a full grown male badger. Justin ran it down and tried to get it by the nape of the neck. For a while, it was hard to tell who had hold of whom. Finally, Justin came up with it by the nape of the neck. The badger was growling, snarling, and trying to twist its head around to get at Justin's hands. He had already almost torn his pants off and had bitten him on the hands and legs. But that made no difference to that brother of mine. He had things under control. When we arrived home and Dad saw the creature Justin was carrying, Dad wanted to get the gun and shoot the animal. After much pleading, Dad finally gave in and the badger was turned loose in the granary. It only took a week for that old badger to chew his way to freedom.

Justin liked jokes. One day on the way to school, he found a large gopher snake. Hiding the snake under his shirt, he took the snake into the school. When he was seated, Justin turned the snake loose in the aisle. That teacher went into a real screaming session until the snake was finally herded out the door. The teacher knew who the culprit was and tried to jerk Justin out of his seat. In doing so, she passed gas in a loud way. The poor gal was in tears.

This poor teacher, Miss Nelson, had a rough time with us boys. The school had a pair of outside toilets. In the winter time she would peek out the door, during the noon hour, to see where we were playing and if it looked clear. Then she would make a mad dash for the toilet. We would pretend that we did not see her. But upon her return, she would have to run a gauntlet of snowballs.

The Joe Moore farm was not a happy place for my parents. The depression had deepened and dry weather had come to stay. There was not enough feed for the livestock. The government furnished cotton seed cake and cracked wheat. It was not enough help. We lost a lot of cattle and sheep. Dad tried everything to save the cattle; even hanging them up in slings when they were too weak to stand. That summer we cut and stacked Russian thistles for feed. The sheep had bloody mouths from this harsh feed, but still kept eating. We ran out of hog feed so Dad had to kill them as they were becoming vicious.

To add to worries, Charley, the sixth child, was badly cut up in a disk. He was a tough little guy and made it through. He had a batch of stitches in his rump. In spite of all of its problems such as rattle snakes, poor land and a mean bull, the Joe Moore farm brought some good. Our second sister, Dorothy, was born. She was one healthy and beautiful baby. Mom was fortunate that she had no problems with this pregnancy. When pregnant, she was knocked flat by the neighbors ram while milking a cow.

One morning when we were getting ready for school, Dad looked out the door and asked, "Did you forget to tie up your horse?" We looked out and standing by the gate was a chestnut horse. When we put him into the barn yard, we discovered he was in sad shape. He had been tangled up in barb wire and was badly cut up. Dad had to sew him up in several places. He also was very thin. We called him Barney. Howard adopted him because he seemed to tolerate Howard better than any one of us. Barney healed up very well and became a beautiful horse, rather high spirited, but a good quarter horse.

Our first Christmas here, Dad presented George with a 22 rifle. I remember it was a Hamilton single shot. Among the things that George shot at was the outdoor privy. He was really scared one time when he realized he had not checked to see if it was occupied. Thank God no one was in it. That incident caused the rifle to be put up.

Duke, our baby bull, had grown up to be a big problem. If it had not been for old Carlo, our faithful dog, the bull would have surely killed someone. Bob and I were about a mile from home one day when old Duke spotted us. We made it to a tree with Duke bellowing and glaring up at us. We started calling Carlo. After a few minutes, Carlo came streaking toward us. Well, old Duke disappeared over the hill with Carlo hanging on to his tail.

The last winter we spent on the John Moore farm, we acquired two mustang colts, Shy and Major. Shy was a sorrel with blond mane and tail, and a white blaze and stocking feet. Major was a strawberry roan. They were two well behaved horses after much petting and attention from the family.

"We are going to move," announced Dad. This time west again—seventy-five miles to the "Old Meade Ranch". Dad loaded Bob,

Charley, Dolores, Dorothy who was just a baby, Mom, and me into the old
Model T Ford and we headed west. A neighbor brought over his truck and
hauled out a milk cow and a crate of chickens for us. Dad returned to the
Moore farm where he, Howard, Justin, and George hauled the furniture in
hay racks and drove the livestock. It took almost two weeks before Dad and
the boys arrived with the cattle. During that time, we had only milk, eggs,
and cracked wheat to live on.

The Meade ranch had a huge barn and a two room tar paper shack for a
house, our home. To this day, I don't understand how Mom survived. Our
nearest neighbor was four miles away, school six and the closest railroad was
seventy-five miles. We had a little town, Strool, which was fourteen miles
away. It was wonderful country to explore. There was even a creek with a
dam between the house and the barn. Coyotes howled at night and even sat
up on the hills and watched us move in. Our dog, old Carlo, made a deadly
error of trying to chase them. Every time he came home well chewed up.

When Dad and the boys showed up with the livestock, old Duke was
not among them. Dad had sold him to a rancher. Dad and the boys went by
Strool with the cattle. Dad bought some groceries there. Pete, the storekeeper,
put in a bag of hard candy. What a treat that was. With the family all in
tack, Justin, George and I started exploring the country. It was June so no
school. There were just miles and miles of emptiness with lots of peaks, hills,
creeks with deep holes, and springs.

Antelopes, jack rabbits, cotton tails and grouse were everywhere. This
was my dream for I was now entrusted with George's 22 Hamilton. I think
I was born to hunt. Every night after school, I would disappear with the
little 22. Mom was very good at cooking cotton tails which I supplied with
pleasure. One night I brought home a very large porcupine that went into
the dinner fare.

School was six miles away. When we did not ride horses, we took a
team and trailer. Howard, Justin, George and I made up half of the school
as there were only eight boys. Poor Mrs. Steinhauser, our teacher, had her
hands full. She lived at the school during the week in the adjoining kitchen
and bedroom. The school was situated in a large prairie dog town. During
the spring and fall, we heard the continuous whistle of prairie dogs. Playing
ball was impossible with losing all the balls down holes. We were allowed
to bring our rifles to school. They had to be unloaded, left in the hall with
our coats, and could not be used on the school yard. Our horse, Shy, was a
stallion. When we rode him to school, he fell in love with one of the other
boy's mare. We were having a great breeding session in the school yard until

the teacher saw it. Mrs. Steinhauser informed us that Shy would not be allowed at school from then on.

The following year the Dansky family moved into the district with three girls of school age. The girls received our constant attention, especially if we could coax them into the barn at noon. Attending school in the winter was a real problem. We had to use a ridge route as the valley snow was too deep. When a storm blew in, we used to head the team and trailer toward home and all of us boys would get under a big horse hide blanket. The only time we had to come out was to open the gates. That team of horses always headed straight home and never let us down.

Winter was real rough on the family and livestock also. We would have to get them all inside the barn to feed them. Drifts were over ten feet high. Once we recorded 43 degrees below zero. Our little house had two stoves that we kept going with lignite coal. Dad had opened up a mine close to our home. It was an open pit mine. He had to move about twelve feet of clay to get to the coal. It was a lot of sweat for both him and the horses. We boys would help. You had to be very careful if your job was to hang on the fresco handle while the team pulled and loaded.

There were many mines in the area. Some were tunnels. George, Justin and I found this old tunnel that had been abandoned. We used to crawl in because the entrance had partially caved in. Once inside, it was real large. We would make torches and have a grand time running and hiding. Now I shudder to think what could have happened if we had run into a pocket of methane gas or had a cave-in.

This was a different country. It was beautiful in the summer, sunny days with buffalo grass waving like a great ocean. There were lots of Indian signs and arrowheads, buffalo bones and abandoned homesteads. Usually, the only signs of these were deep wells and mounds of sod where the houses once were. I remember one well that was so deep that when we dropped a rock, it would whistle before hitting the bottom with a dry thud. The canyons were full of wild plums and choke cherries. Mom was always happy when we brought a batch home. The plums and cherries made wonderful jelly and jam.

Prairie fires were always a danger in the summer. I remember one that really caused some concern. We could see the smoke south of the ranch early in the morning. That afternoon, the wind changed to the south and the fire came over the hill right toward the ranch. Dad had a team of horses hooked up to the walking plow and tried to outflank the fire. It was moving too fast to get ahead of. We four boys had a stone bolt with a barrel of water hooked up to another team. Using wet burlap bags, we kept the side fires under control. We saved the ranch. That fire burned until it got to the Grand River which was about fifteen miles away.

A quite different visitor to our ranch was Buck, a half breed Indian (according to Mom and Dad). Dad was very protective of Buck, especially when the county sheriff would show up and inquire if anyone had seen Buck. I guess Buck did something outside the law; but Dad would not reveal it to us. He would always tell the sheriff that Buck had not been around. Buck always helped Dad when it was needed.

Buck was a real cowboy and could ride anything that walked. One day he brought the wild horses that roamed the ranch into the corral. As us boys watched, he roped a beautiful steel blue mare. We were amazed how he hog tied the horse. He then put the saddle and bridles on. While getting on the horse, Buck yelled at us to open the gate. He then pulled the rope loose so the horse could get up. That mare went out of the gate bucking and bellowing with Buck on top. They ran over the hill and out of sight. That afternoon Buck came back with that horse as gentle as a lamb. One day when Buck was down by the corral, George asked him if he ever threw the knife that he carried on his belt. Buck told George to mark off a spot on the barn door. Well a knife ended up in the spot, but it was not the knife from his belt. It was the one that came from behind his neck.

During the spring, us boys earned money snaring gophers and collecting baby crow and magpie heads. The county paid us five cents for each gopher tail and ten cents for each crow or magpie head. The gopher tails were easy to keep. Although we packed them in salt, the heads smelled real bad by the time we got them to the county office. Ten cents for the heads was real money at that time. Dad would go along with us to help collect our bounty. It always amazed me that the county was so worried about a few gophers in those days. The animal that did the real damage was the prairie dog.

I often wonder how Mom survived the Meade Ranch being so far from a doctor or any medical help. There was the time when Justin spilled a cup of coffee on little Dolores and scalded her whole chest. I remember so well how she screamed and cried for two days. Dad went to the nearest neighbor and borrowed some antiseptic powder. Mom pulled Dolores through; but to this day she still carries those scars. A doctor later told Mom that he could not understand how she lived. Then there were scarlet fever, mumps, measles, chicken pox, and so on. Mom always got out the big doctor book when any sickness or injury happened. We were lucky that none of the boys ever got shot or snake bite. When it came to snake bite, it could have easily happened as I had a cigar box full of rattles from the snakes that I had killed. As for broken bones, we took our chances. Every Sunday our main pastime was to round up some steers for bareback riding. George had one black steer that must have weighed close to 600 pounds. He could ride that old steer to a complete standstill.

I herded cattle for Mr. Sandford one summer for two dollars a week. It was my first experience with adult sex. Mr. Humphrey, who lived about a mile from Sandford's, usually came over for breakfast. Mr. Sanford was many years older than his wife who was very heavy. As usual, Mr. Sanford and I left the house to gather up the cattle. I remembered that I had forgotten my water bottle and returned to the house. What a surprise! There was Mrs. Sandford with no clothes and Mr. Humphrey taking his off. It took me a long time to figure out just what was taking place. I never mentioned this to anyone for fear of Mr. Humphrey. I was lucky that I was able to sneak out without them seeing me. I made enough money that summer to answer my dream. Mom bought the material and made me a two-tone cowboy shirt. With new jeans, boy I was sharp.

If we had not been able to mine all the coal we needed, there would have been a very small chance of surviving the cold winters. One night it was 43 degrees below zero. Our little house, without any kind of insulation or inside sheathing, was little protection against the cold. We had only two rooms with a stove in each. Every night we had to put up beds which were stored in a lean-to. The last winter, we moved over to the ranch where Mr. and Mrs. Meade lived. We were crowded, but warm as this was a sod house.

Little Charley started school and proved to be a real tough guy. We older boys misused him at times just for a laugh. Anytime he was hurt, we would say, "Call it a joke Charley." Many times with tears in his eyes he would say, "Joke." Bobby received his share of abuse by his older brothers also. He had a habit of smarting off at us older boys and then running for his mother. Anytime we could catch him, it was into the dam. He says to this day that is where he learned to walk on water.

One day Dad told us boys that we would soon have another member added to our family. Being the older boys, we knew that this was coming. We acted surprised anyway—just to show our innocence. We all hoped for a sister because we already had enough brothers.

The day arrived so Dolores and Dorothy were sent to the neighbors and us boys were told to stay in the barn. About noon, the neighbor lady rode in on horseback. It was about two hours later when we heard a baby crying. We knew our new member of the family had arrived. Dad came down to the barn and announced, "You have a new baby sister." She was named Alice Lorraine.

In spite of all the hard times, cold weather, shortages of food, and long distance to school, the country excited me. I loved roaming the hills, creeks, and valleys with my little single shot twenty-two. I especially loved the rim rock on the hills. My name and the date are still carved in the ceiling of a sandstone cave that I found. I loved all the nature with the chatter of the magpies in the canyons, the lonely whistle of the curlew, and the barking whistle of the prairie dogs. Coyotes were always present but kept their distance. In the mornings and evenings, they serenaded everyone.

*Henry Johnson Family 1924*

On Uncle Bill's Farm 1931

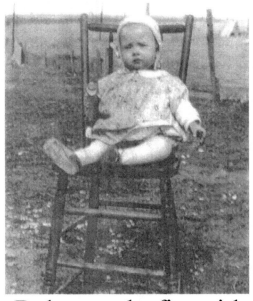

Dolores – the first girl

# CHAPTER 2

## Lake Preston

## 1933—1941

The years did not improve. The depression was already hurting everybody and then came the drought. Dad decided that we had to move back to Mom's old home in Lake Preston. Uncle Carl had written that Gramma Setbacken was failing and needed help. Mom, Bob, Charley, Dolores, Dorothy, Lorraine, and I went by train. Howard, Justin, and George stayed with Dad to sell the sheep and drive the cattle to Hettinger, North Dakota. The government was buying the cattle at fifteen dollars a head. The cattle were shot and buried in a large trench. It was a sad situation. But if not that, they would have starved. Dad told us later that in the drive to Hettinger several ranches went together so they had a very large number of cattle. He said that they left a 75 mile trail of dead cattle because so many were too weak. Howard and Justin arrived in Lake Preston, and then Dad and George arrived two weeks later.

Leonard was born at the Setbacken Farm, which meant so much to Mom. He brought the family up to seven boys and three girls. Howard, Justin, and George finished school in Perkins County so the four next younger ones attended our little rural school. It was very similar to the one out West. The main difference was there were more children. All eight grades were taught by one teacher. Life here was very enjoyable. All the boys carried slingshots so there were very few insulators left on the telephone poles. Occasionally a shot gun shell dropped into the school furnace and added a little excitement. As the school had no barn, the games between the boys and girls kept in the school yard were not like the ones played out West.

The Setbacken farm had many areas to explore. The house was big and roomy with three rooms upstairs for us boys. The barn had a hay loft with a track and hay hoist that us boys could really ride on. There was also a granary with lots of grain bins, a hog house and a chicken house. The main interest was an old shop with all kinds of black smith tools including a forge and a huge anvil for making all kinds of things. Behind the shop was a pile of car parts, old machinery, and many other items. The farm had 160 acres of land with a creek running through. There was also a large slough right behind the house that kept water the year round. There were lots of ducks, muskrats, and loads of frogs.

Mom was in her glory. She had a piano again, a real kitchen and a bedroom for just her and Dad. What a treat it must have been for her to be able to visit with the neighboring ladies in town after all the years of loneliness she suffered out west. She and Dad even started attending dances on Saturday nights with friends.

Moving from western South Dakota to the eastern part of the state made quite a difference. Our closest neighbor out West was three miles away, our school five miles, and our little town fourteen miles. There was loads of open country to explore. Here the town was just three miles away and would make ten of our little town out West. Our school and many neighbors were less than a mile away. We had only 160 acres to roam on so privacy was gone. Howard found a job away from home. Justin took off for the nearest carnival. Therefore George and I had to entertain ourselves.

George was down behind the old shop one day when he called, "Herbert, I found something we can make into a cannon." It was an old drive housing about five feet long and tapered down with a grease cup fitting in the lower end. As it was spring and the geese were flying north very high. This would be the gun that could reach them. Dad always had a keg of black powder in the granary so we had the firepower. It took a little while to construct a make-shift tripod for pointing the cannon to the heavens. Then we put a fuse through the grease cup hole, a lot of black powder, wadding, and then nuts and bolts to fill it. We were sitting there with match in hand waiting for the next flock of geese when Uncle Carl came upon us. "What in the hell are you two doing with that powder keg?" Well when he spotted our gun, our day's shoot was off. In fact, all shoots were off forever.

Several months passed since our dismal failure with the goose shoot. Dad let us go out in the pasture and help with blowing up stumps. We learned how to drill the hole, and insert the fuse and black powder. We considered ourselves experts. One day Dad said, "You two want to go to town with me?"

"No, we will stay home with Mom." As soon as Dad cleared the driveway, George said, "Let's blow up that big stump behind the barn." We headed to the granary for the keg of black powder. George was drilling the powder hole with the hand auger when he said, "this stump is hollow. Will that make a difference?" I assured him that it would be O.K. It seemed like it took a lot of powder to pack that stump. Finally we filled the hole, put in our fuse, and packed it with mud like Dad showed us.

Luck was with the two of us. We retreated behind a large log some distance from the stump after we lit the fuse. Well, there was quite an explosion! The stump disappeared in a flash of fire and smoke. The windows in the barn and granary all broke out. The cistern way up by the house cracked. Dad stopped on his way home to talk with Leroy Wink who lived about three quarters of a mile up the road. They both heard the loud whoop, and saw the dust and smoke rise above the tree line. When Dad came home, he totally convinced the two of us that we would leave the black powder alone.

I've often wondered how Mom survived us boys. There was the cold winter day Mom found Bob and I down by the barn throwing frozen horse terds at anything that moved. Bob had gone into the barn when I noticed the neighbor's old tom cat that had a reputation of killing kittens. I picked up this good horse terd and let it fly. At just that moment, Bob came out of the barn and that missile hit him in the back of the head. He went down in a heap. I ran over to him. Shaking had no effect so I headed for the house. "Mom! I just killed Bob." Poor Mom ran for the barn with me following. When we arrived, Bob was sitting up with a look that said, "What happened?" It took a while for both of us to recover.

I was introduced to high school and the John Lawler Pool Hall the following year. My grades in high school were just passing, but no one could touch me in snooker at the pool hall. I skipped school one morning and was playing Dave Patterson, the town shark, when I happened to look over at the side. There sat Dad with a smile on his face. Thank heaven I was beating Old Dave badly or my dad would not have been smiling. He just said, "You get back to school."

At school, I met my dearest friend, Leroy Stephens. We planned a way to make money buying and selling potatoes. We had to buy them from the Mennonites at Lake Norden, about twenty miles from Lake Preston. We had to haul the potatoes at night and sell them by the sack at school. On one night haul, we lost our trailer on a curve. We were almost home before we noticed the trailer was missing. Luckily it was upright and the potatoes still in tack.

The following spring we made enough money to buy seed potatoes. Our neighbor donated to us five acres of land he was not using. We were set to be potato farmers. Dad furnished the equipment to plow and plant. We did the hoeing. Leroy and I used to go out by the field and sit and dream of all the money we were about to make. All the conditions for a good crop existed until two weeks before digging. Then the grasshoppers moved in and stripped the plants to the ground. What a let down. When we did dig our potatoes, they were a little larger than a golf ball. Leroy and I hauled these small potatoes by the sack all over the county and sold them for two dollars a sack. I think we broke about even on the whole adventure.

Leroy and I had good times together. Mom loved to accompany him on the piano when he sang Danny Boy. We dated two sisters. He eventually married his date. As for me, I was scared off by a too aggressive girl. When the war broke out, Leroy was assigned to a bomber group as a tail gunner. His plane went down over Greece. I always felt so bad that he never saw his little "Danny Boy" that was born after he left.

Another good friend that I met in Lake Preston was Jasper Thompson. Jasper was from a real German family with sauerkraut by the barrel in the basement, home cured hams and a real hard working and prosperous farm. He raised brown homing pigeons which really excited me. After a few trips and a little money, I was the owner of two pairs. I built a home for them in the straw loft over the chicken house. After two years, my flock had grown to several pairs. Tragedy hit my flock in the form of a tom cat and I was back to two pairs. A fool proof home had to be built for my flock. It all started with four ash poles set in the ground with the height of about ten feet. It was on top of these poles that I erected my new home for my pigeons. I remember Dad saying this was a poor idea. "First storm and you won't have anything left." Many years later when I visited the old farm, all that was left was part of the barn and my pigeon house. Jasper and I hunted and trapped together. We even had a trap line that we would check on the way to school. We gave this up after catching our first skunk and with the strong persuasion of the principal.

High school was rather a hardship for me. It should have not been. The combination of my desire to play pool, being too short to make the basketball team, being extremely shy, and Miss Hansee shaking her head when I tried out for the Glee Club made life a little tough at times. The music teacher, Mr. Hammond, was my biggest problem. He stopped me several times when I was sneaking out of school to play pool. The worst incident was my last year. Our assembly room had large windows in front covered with shades. About every month I would give them a whack with a rubber band fitted with a piece of tin foil. When I sat in the back of the room, I had no problem. The last year, I let go of one and a hand hit me in the back of the head. Mr. Hammond said, "Johnson, I've been looking for you for the last two years. I was expelled for two days.

Although my grades in high school always needed improvement, one subject that I always kept very good grades in. It was Manual Training, or shop. Jack Ryder was the shop teacher and was very good with his students. I picked out a spinning wheel lamp for my first year project. The spinning wheel would only be about twelve inches, but had to be operable. Mr. Ryder told me it was a good choice, but very time consuming with almost precision work. It took two years to complete the lamp with the little delicate spinning wheel. Mom was so pleased when I gave it to her. I had a lot of respect for Jack Ryder.

My next project was for Dad. Dad had always had to make do with rather poor farm equipment. I had heard him mention that he really needed a gang drag. There was a lot of old equipment around the farm. Upon checking it out, I found sections of drags that had been abandoned due to oak beams rotting out. When my grandfather came back from Indiana, he brought quite a supply of oak which he used around the farm. I talked to Mr. Ryder to see if it was possible to build a gang drag in class. With his encouragement, I started on the project. It was the spring of my senior year when I finished that drag. I will always remember how pleased Dad was when I brought home that drag all painted bright red. Years later when he had his farm sale, Dad told me that the drag brought top dollar.

In thinking back over all the years, Mom and Dad sure did not demand a lot from life. We had picnics at some lake or in the town park. A great time was Saturday night in town when Mom could get a dish of ice cream, and Dad would have a few beers and play pool. With all the strain of a large family, hard times, and weather that could make havoc with the crops, I wonder how they kept smiling. They had one thing going strong for them, love. They were very much in love with each other.

Growing up, every child should have a favorite pet. I was very fortunate to have mine. His name was Nickey, my pet crow. I found Nickey when he was acquiring feathers. I spotted his nest while out hunting gophers. When I climbed the tall tree, there in the nest were two baby crows, Nickey, the largest, and his small roommate. I took them both home, much to the disgust of Mom and Dad, and announced that I was going to raise them. Nickey readily took to hand feeding of bread and milk, but his little nest mate refused and therefore died. As Nickey grew, he decided that I was his mom. He would follow me around the farm doing his best to fly. It was a great day for both of us the day that he flew up and landed on my shoulder. He would put his bill in my ear and make quiet little crow talk.

Nickey loved to tease and the cats were his favorite victims. When spotting a cat, he would fly and land real close. The cats would do their best to catch him. It was to no avail because Nickey kept out of their reach. The minute the cat would get tired and start walking away, he would have it by the tail. Nickey also loved shiny objects such as pennies, cup handles, and small tools. One day Dad was working on the tractor and laid down a small wrench. Nickey had it and went off to the rain gutter where he stored his keepsakes. Every so often I would get the ladder and recover his loot. I was painting the house one day. Nickey was there along side giving me some trouble so I patted him on the head with the paint brush containing green paint. Well, Nickey carried a green head for about two months.

Nickey shared the farm for over two years. He became very popular with the neighborhood so we had many visitors. The Huron Zoo heard about him and came to the farm in an attempt to buy him. I did not want to part with Nickey so I turned down their offer. That might have been a mistake. Nickey's downfall was to his favorite habit of picking grasshoppers out of car radiators. He spotted this car a couple hundred yards down the road. Well, the car contained pheasant hunters who just shot another damn crow.

Halloween was an exciting time in Lake Preston because all the young people always gathered together to pull off a big surprise. One Halloween night about forty of us, mostly high school students, brought three thrashing machines to Main Street. We pulled them in to town by hand. Pete Oggard, the town marshal, tried to stop us, but ended up almost being run over. The following Halloween, we came up with another stunt. A contractor was doing some cement work at the high school and had a large pile of sand. We found a wagon nearby and dismantled it. Then, piece by piece, we carried it up to the roof of the high school where we reassembled it. We then formed a bucket brigade and filled it with sand. It took a crew of men to undo our little deal. There was one good thing about this group of kids. We were so busy pulling off some stunt that we did not have time for Halloween vandalism.

# CHAPTER 3

## Young Adventures

## 1933—1941

Chink Eykamp, Milton Strande, and I ran around together. Milton did not attend high school due to his being abused by a step dad. Chink and I both had motorcycles. His was a new Indian Scout. Mine was an old Harley 74 that I bought for fifteen dollars. Uncle Carl had a shop in town. With his assistance, it became a real cycle.

The sheriff in DeSmet, a neighboring town, had a new Ford car which we heard could outrun anything on the highway. Well, Chink and I fired up our cycles and headed for DeSmet. We slowly rode up the main road and spotted the sheriff and his new car in front of the barber shop. He was sitting in front on a bench and eyeballed us as we rode slowly by. When we came to the end of the street, we turned around and opened up the cycles to roar by. We headed for the highway as he jumped into his car. Well I hit a speed of 100 miles per hour on my speedometer and Chink on his Scout was gaining on me. The sheriff's siren slowly lost its sound behind us. The fact that Dad found out about it surprised me. He just said, "Put that cycle in the granary." He sold it later when I went into the Navy.

Graduation Day finally arrived. I was the lowest in my class of 33 in grade average, but no one could touch me at John Lawler's Pool Hall. That June, Milt and I decided to go west. Howard, Justin, and George had all been out West and had great stories about all the work to be found. The freight train out of Lake Preston was our choice. When we reached the main line at Bristol, we found the trains were full of riders all heading west. This trip grew both of us up in a hurry. Life aboard a train was not all pleasure as we had thought. On the train, we met a fellow about thirty who took us under his wing for two days. We were in this box car when this character spotted Milt and I. Not knowing that we had our protector with us, he started to crawl into the car. This fellow kicked the character right in the face. He then told us that this type would kill for pennies and do us bodily harm. He said we should never travel alone in any box cars. Our protector had ridden freight trains for years.

This man also showed us how to bum food off the locals. At one stop, Milt took off to see if he could round up some food. The train took off before he returned. I thought we had finally been split up when I heard him hollering from on top of the box car. Luckily we had several fellows in the car and were able to pull him down into it. He had a huge bag of sandwiches.

We arrived in Ellensburg several days later. After cleaning up at the stockyard water tank, we headed out of town to look for Milton's relatives, Theodore, Oscar and Bertha Strande. Once we located them, we were treated to a great meal, bunk house and jobs. Milt and I worked for these Strandes for several months. It is here I shot my first elk. I had sent home for the old black powder and used that to hunt with. We were up in the mountains in the snow when I saw this bull with a bunch of cows. I shot him seven times before he fell. Milt was about a mile away. He said that at one time there were six puffs of smoke rising in the cold air. The old 44 had a lot of fire but not much punch.

After working for the Strandes, Milt and I decided to look up some of my relatives. I had Aunt and Uncle Anderson who lived at Sela, about forty miles away. When we hitchhiked to Longmire Dairy where Oscar worked, we were told there was quite a bit of work. My cousin, Margaret, who was my age, immediately fell in love with Milt. This did not set well with Oscar. Margaret was his step daughter. I found out later that he had his eye on her himself.

Milt and I helped around the dairy and also started to pick potatoes. What a hell of a job. We were paid five cents per sack so it was daylight to dark in order to make five dollars a day. After two days picking, we both had charley horses in our legs so bad we could hardly walk. One of the old pickers told us to use liniment to rub down our legs at night. I lay on my stomach and Milt rubbed me down first. Then it was his turn. I was rubbing his legs down when I happened to splash some liniment in his butt. Well, I have never seen anyone without pants make it to the water tank that fast.

Milt and I were thinning pears one day and working on 11 foot ladders when I found this extremely large pear. I tossed it in the general direction of Milt and hollered, "Look at this one Milt." Then I heard a loud crash and turned to see Milt under his ladder with half the tree on top of him. He later said I had hit him right on top of his head. No broken bones so we just laughed it off.

In the fall we decided to move back to the Strande Ranch. I had a job of plowing with a cat and Milt herded cattle. We went deer and elk hunting here. Christmas was getting close so we decided to head for home. This time we bought tickets on the passenger train. Boy, were we proud. The two of us had new cowboy hats, leather jackets, western boots, and money in our pockets. I even had purchased a portable typewriter. We arrived in Lake Preston in style.

Lake Preston soon became a drag at my age so I looked for something to change the scenery. Milt, Chink and I decided to go rabbit hunting in the western part of the state, especially where the old Meade Ranch was located. Milt had a Dodge coup which we rigged with two spot lights. We borrowed my Dad's two wheeled trailer. With three 22's, lots of ammunition, some food, blankets, and not too much money, we headed west. It was the first of November with no snow on the ground. The rabbits showed up because they had already turned white for winter. We started hunting as soon as we crossed the Missouri River. All our hunting was done at night. We often left the roads and headed across the open prairie with the North Star for a compass.

Out in the middle of a lot of emptiness, we spotted a water tank and pulled up to it. The farmer came out to see just who we were. He was very happy to give us some water. While we were watering up the old Dodge, rats kept coming up to the water tank. I asked the farmer why he did not get rid of some of the rats. His answer was, "If you boys will stick around tonight and shoot rats, I'll give you the best breakfast you ever ate in the morning." As hungry as we were for some good home cooked food, we stayed and shot rats all night long. In the morning, we had a huge pile of rats by that water tank. The breakfast was really a wonderful experience.

After many miles of towing, the tires on the trailer gave out and we pulled into this little town on rims. Just as we were leaving we noticed this little travel trailer with balloon tires on the same size of wheels. This trailer was up on blocks so temptation hit us. We parked about a half mile outside of town. When it was dark, we walked, crawled and sneaked into town. Soon the new tires were put on our trailer and the old wheels were left. I am sure we must have driven fifty miles before we stopped for the night. Then I felt the whole South Dakota police force was out combing the country for us. When we finally got back home, I told Dad that we bought the tires. Many years later he told me he knew we had gotten those tires by some other means. I was never very proud of this action and wished over the years that I would have been able to compensate the owner.

After being out in the country for three weeks, Chink came down with a fever so we headed home. By the time we were half way home, Chink was so sick that we had to pull into a small town and find a doctor. The doctor put him into bed and said he had rabbit fever. Milt and I headed home while Chink's dad came after him.

# CHAPTER 4

## The War Years
## 1941—1946

I remember the telephone jingling the ring that meant everyone was supposed to pick up the receiver because there was an important message concerning all phone owners. The operator in a very nervous voice told us that Pearl Harbor had been attacked by the Japanese. We had to find a world map to locate Pearl Harbor. A few nights later President Roosevelt was on the radio with a message to the American people. The one passage that stood out was, "We have nothing to fear but fear itself."

I decided to volunteer so Dad took me to Huron, which was about forty miles away, to sign up. I wanted to join the air force. We discovered the office was closed when we arrived at the federal building. I inquired, at the office across the hall, as to when they would be in. This was the Navy Recruiting Office. Yes, you might have guessed it. Five minutes later, I was signed up for the Navy.

There were so many volunteers signing up that when we finally arrived at the Great Lakes Naval Training Station, there were not enough facilities to handle us all. We were shipped south to New Orleans to get us out of the January cold. I will always remember leaving the snow and cold of Chicago and waking up on the train the next morning to see everything so green. Upon arriving at the Alameda Naval Training Station, I found myself in the same confusion as at Great Lakes. There were not enough barracks or dining space available.

It was decided that we would be put out on quarters and subsistence in private homes or boarding houses. My group was assigned to the Degaussing Department. This was the treating of ships for magnetic mines. This station was located on the Mississippi River across from New Orleans. Our stations consisted of two large barges. We located boarding in an apartment house in town close to the dock that would take us to our duty each day.

One result of the confusion with the large number of volunteers was that our group had no military training. Some of our uniforms had been issued to us. But there was no gunnery practice or instructions. We found ourselves in the Navy from eight in the morning to four in the afternoon. We even had to pack our lunches. Having liked office work and typing, I was picked by the officer in charge to do the record keeping. After about six months, they opened up another station. Then I was assigned a station wagon and a speed boat to cover both stations.

New Orleans was an exciting city to this country boy with its bars in the French Quarters, brothels everywhere, race track, street cars, winding streets, and different food. The girls were beautiful and friendly. My landlady, Julie, kept me on the right track. She was an excellent cook. I enjoyed many good meals in her company. Life was good to me in New Orleans. I was granted permission to be able to check out any vehicle at anytime at the Navy vehicle pool. A speed boat was assigned to me for hauling crew members to our deperming barge on the island in the Miswasu Canal.

While staying at 1035 Jefferson I met my good friend, Bob Doyle. After about two months, Bob's sweetheart, Dottie, arrived and plans were under way for a wedding. I was Bob's best man. The three of us became acquainted with another good friend, Melvin Sergeant. He was a civilian employee of the Navy.

I used to catch crabs out of the canal and bring them back to Julie. What a feast we would have—crabs on the half shell with lots of wine. The two of us would really have a party. One day after a real good catch of crabs, I had so many that I put them in a gunny sack to take home. I had not checked out a car that day so I had to take them home on the street car. Those little blue crabs are real ornery critters and in no time I had claws sticking out of that gunny sack on the street car. Everyone sure gave me a wide berth.

I had a very close call with fire at 1035 Jefferson. My room was upstairs in the back of the house. It had an outside door that led to a small porch. I had gone to bed and left the little gas heater going because it was a cold January night. It was the grace of God that woke me in a complete daze. It felt like someone was standing on my chest and I could not breathe. While struggling, I fell out of bed. Apparently, the air was better there. I then realized the room was full of smoke. I groped around the room on my hands and knees and finally found the outside door. My pea coat had fallen from the foot of my bed onto the gas heater and caught fire. No other part of the room was burning. It was just a matter of throwing the burning coat out in the back yard. I was very fortunate.

New Orleans was my introduction to horse racing. My first trip was with a pharmacist mate who was more experienced with racing. He talked me into betting a ten dollar parlay. The first race my horse came sailing in. The next race I had parlayed was in the fifth. This race ended up in a photo finish. To my great enjoyment, I was the winner. We both guessed that I had won over eighty dollars. When I went to the cashier, I learned we were way off as he laid down three hundred dollar bills plus forty-five dollars in front of me. I paid for the party at the little tavern that night.

One night I was put in charge of the watch at the nine mile point deperming station. This could only be reached by boat. I had four seamen under my charge. We all had to carry a 38 caliber pistol while on watch. I had given all the usual instructions about not removing the pistol from the holster. You only removed it if you were going to use it in case of emergency or for protection. Willy had the last four o'clock to eight o'clock watch. He came into the bunk room to wake us. He pointed the pistol at me and clicked the trigger on an empty chamber. He then turned toward Holtz. I shouted at him to stop it just as the gun went off shooting Holtz through the shoulder. After calling the shore patrol for a boat, I went back to the back bunk. There on Willy's bunk lay five shells. One had stuck in the chamber. I felt sorry for Holtz, but thanked God I had not been the one to take the shot.

I acquired a real pet the last year before departing New Orleans. She was a little brown and white terrier which I called Flash, after the Flashing Station. She was a natural seaman. She rode on the bow of the speed boat and loved a little sailing skiff I had made. We spent many days sailing up and down the canal. About a month before my transfer, the crew wanted to keep her overnight at the station. Somehow she was run over when they took her along for show. What a loss.

I had a real good commanding officer, Lieutenant Morgan. He gave me a rating increase before I left so I was now second class yeoman. He could not understand why I wanted to leave when I had such a good deal. I had been in New Orleans for over a year and wanted to see something different. I had checked out the rating request at Ninth Naval Headquarters and found that a second class yeoman was needed in Clarksville, Arkansas. They were converting the College of the Ozarks to a radio school. I took leave to go home before reporting to the school. It was good to see the folks and I enjoyed my two weeks with them. Howard was in Alaska. Justin was somewhere out West. George had been turned down by the Army because of a bad heart so he had gone to California. Lake Preston, my old home town, was not the same with so many of my friends in the service. My younger brother, Charles, had been injured in an automobile accident so I stayed home for the full two weeks and helped Dad with the harvest.

Racial discrimination, as we know it, was only referred to as "the damn niggers" when I arrived in New Orleans. There were white and black toilets and drinking fountains. There were even signs that read, "No Blacks." It was hard for a Yankee boy to understand. Back home, we had a black family in our neighborhood and they caused no special attention. I don't remember any ill feelings about them living in the area. My first real contact in New Orleans came one evening while riding home on the St. Charles street car. When I got aboard, there were several blacks standing up in the rear of the car. I could not understand why. Then I noticed a sign with the words "No Blacks Forward" was on the back of the last seat. Without a thought of any problem, I walked back and moved the sign forward as half of the street car was empty. The conductor, a very big and burly character, stopped the street car and came back to where I was seated. "Boy, where are you from?" I said, "South Dakota." His words were something like, "Yankee, you put that sign back where you got it. Any more of this and you will be walking."

At the first boarding house in New Orleans, we were all unpacking when a young and rather good looking black girl came into the room to check out the towels and bed clothes. One of our groups was a native of New Orleans. He looked at the girl and in a voice she could plainly hear said, "Would you guys like a little of that stuff?" She turned and with a scared look on her face said, "Please don't do it to me." He later bragged about a Saturday night entertainment of picking up black girls forcibly and gang banging them. I asked him about getting into trouble with the law. His answer was, "No problem as long as it was with black girls."

How easy it is to become brainwashed. I had been down South only a little over a year when I went home on leave. After changing trains in Minneapolis for Sioux Falls, the train I boarded had only one seat left. A black sailor occupied the seat next to it. Rather than sit with him, I stood up. I wish I knew his name and how to contact him. I would like to apologize still today.

When I arrived at Clarksville and reported at the College of the Ozarks, I met Commander Gatley. I was assigned to be his writer. My desk was right outside his office so I was at his beckoned call. This gave me a position of prestige even with the junior officers. No one could see Commander Gatley without seeing me first. I was a member of all the inspection teams and present at any event the commander attended. I always made sure no one entered his domain without my announcement. He told me that this was what he liked in a writer. When I left there, I received a commendation in my personnel record that really helped me later.

Clarksville was definitely a "small town." Their main industry was mining. The locals were hard to get to know at first, but slowly thawed out. I was invited to dinner with one of the families and had a real good time. The next day being Sunday, their daughter wanted me to take a ride out in the country to visit her grandparents. It was a typical mountain cabin and barn right on top of a hill. When we arrived by horseback, her grandfather was in the barn milking the cows. I asked if I could help him. He looked very distasteful at me and said, "You're a sailor boy and you think you can milk a cow?" Well, when I finished the second one in front of him, he changed his whole attitude. After dinner he excused himself and came back with a jug of white lightening or real Arkansas moonshine. We had a good visit and I spent the night. The next morning, we took a horseback ride further back into the hills. I felt very uncomfortable with the cold stares of the locals we passed. Not even a hello in response to our greeting.

At the base, everything had settled into a routine. Then one day I was looking over the request for personnel. Camp Wallace in Texas boot camp was being commissioned and they needed a yeoman second class. I asked Commander Gatley for a transfer because I wanted to get back to more activity. My request was granted and I was off for Texas.

When I arrived, the personnel officer asked me to accompany three other petty officers on a trip to Memphis Tennessee. We needed to pick up four station wagons for the station. What a trip. I had expense money, a day layover in Memphis, and an extra day traveling time. Memphis was a real treat. Service men could do no wrong in any of the numerous nightclubs. Girls were friendly and made our stay wonderful. There was more to see when we got back. Houston was a few miles to the north and Galveston a few miles to the south.

Camp Wallace was also a prisoner of war camp. Every evening, the German prisoners put on a concert in their camp. They were sure treated well which is something they did not share with our prisoners of war. While at Camp Wallace, I had my second leave. While on leave one Saturday night, I visited my old home town of Lake Preston. Some of my old friends wanted to know where I had been. Two of my old classmates were in uniform decorated with ribbon. I sure did not feel proud of myself, riding the gravy train for two years. Arriving back in Camp Wallace, I went straight to the personnel officer with a request that I be shipped out. "Johnson," he said, "Are you crazy? You can ride out the war right here." At my insistence, he agreed that I should report to the Alameda Naval Station for further orders. He had a draft of two enlisted men and four waves to take to the same station. He put me in charge which was almost my undoing. As New Orleans was my old stomping grounds and I typed up my own orders, I did not put a time of arrival or report in at New Orleans. We left in the morning and arrived that night. With the O.K. of my draft, we checked into a hotel for the night. Then it was a party and an evening on the town. Arriving at the gate to Alameda Naval Station the next morning, we were greeted by a spit and polish second lieutenant. "Johnson, you are thirteen hours AWOL in charge of a draft. Report to the legal officer."

I went over to the Legal Office and asked the yeoman on duty what the problem was. He told me that the transportation receipt had arrived and had no "delay en route" on it. I asked him to give it to me and just turn his back for a minute. I endorsed it "delay en route" authorized and signed it W. H. Green, Capt. USN. When I was called before the Legal Officer, he told me that he could see no problem as I had a delay authorized by the Commandant of Camp Wallace. The lieutenant knew I had pulled a fast one on him and was gunning for me the next liberty. He caught me with tailor made blues on as I was going out the gate. Well, I found myself cutting up my sixty dollar suit and patrolling the clothes line with a dummy rifle that evening instead of going on liberty.

I knew I was dead if I stayed at that base so over to the personnel office to see what I could find to get the hell out of this place and overseas. They needed a yeoman for a heavy cruiser being launched at Norfolk and a yeoman was needed for a Yard Mine Sweeper, YMS, which was tied up at this base. I asked for orders to the YMS 363. When I reported on board, I found out to my pleasure that it was leaving in the morning for my old deperming station. Then we were headed for Panama and the Pacific. We used to kid one another when I was stationed on the deperming station that if you did not shape up we would ship you out on a YMS. Well you can just imagine the hoop la la I received when we pulled into the deperming station and there was Johnson on a Yard Mine Sweeper.

Panama was exciting with tropical waters and jungles. We arrived at the north end of the canal. Colon was a town of bars and prostitutes. Trobaugh and I went swimming in a pool on the base without getting permission so we were confined to the ship for three days. Captain Nicholas finally gave us liberty on the last day so to town we went. Trobaugh decided to get plastered and decided to run with me in pursuit. We finally had some MP's chasing the two of us. When we finally made it to the ship, the MP's had lost us. They started a ship to ship hunt for us. We had gotten muddy crawling under a fence and they knew it. We took all our clothes including shoes and dropped them overboard attached to a three inch shell. Luck was with us. After a few questions, they left. They did not know we had brought back a load of booze which was stored down in the bilges.

The day before we left Colon Panama, three marine sergeants came aboard and announced that the whole crew would be taken out for gunnery testing. We were taken out to a beach some distance where they had two twenty millimeter guns set up. An airplane towing a sleeve would make a pass for each man to try to hit the sleeve which was quite a distance behind the plane. As I was one of the last to try out, I could see that everyone was shooting behind the sleeve. When it was my turn, the old sergeant said, "I see you have been watching pretty closely. Do you see the mistake?" I said, "They are not leading enough." "Well, try to correct that." I gave that sleeve a good lead. What a satisfaction when it started to smoke. He turned to the captain and said, "Put this man on the twenty." Captain Nicholas responded, "His rate does not qualify for gunnery." "That makes no difference to us. He is a good gunner so use him." I guess I was the only yeoman in the Navy that got a chance to shoot a twenty millimeter.

From Panama City we headed for the nearest land fall. This was Ukaheva which was about fifteen sailing days west. The seas were calm. The P.A. system played the most recent hit, "When My Sugar Walks Down The Street." We had gunnery practice almost daily. I was surprised that with my rate I was assigned to the twenty millimeter as assistant gunner and loader. Our practice really paid off in the future. The three inch crew was getting in good shape.

Our Yard Mine Sweeper, YMS, was 130 feet in length and a 36 foot beam. They were originally built for use in coastal waters. Armament included one three inch gun, two single twenties, two twin fifties, two Y guns and racks for depth charges. Top speed on the two diesels was ten knots. The YMS's were not made for extended oversea use as they lacked storage space.

We had twenty-seven enlisted men and three officers. I soon found out the crew was very friendly and easy to get acquainted with. My job as ship's writer gave me a little office for my desk and files. All enlisted men slept below on cots hanging from the overhang on chains. The two chiefs had separate quarters below well separated from the rest of the crew. Officers slept in their quarters topside.

After about ten days sailing, we approached the Equator which is a very important crossing in every Navy man's day. Part of the crew members were Shellback or those who had crossed before. The rest of us were Pollywogs who needed to be changed to Shellbacks. All of us Pollywogs were stripped down to our shorts. The chief boatswain mate became King Neptune at whose throne we had to kneel. Upon kneeling we were given a poke in the butt with his pitchfork and the pad we knelt on was wired. The next event was crawling through a twenty foot long canvas shoot filled with motor oil and overripe garbage. In the shoot, we had to keep moving as the Shellbacks beat on us. When through the shoot, we were hosed down and told we could beat on the next people in the shoot because we were now official Shellbacks. All three officers had to go through this also as they were Pollywogs. I did not realize how serious the Navy takes this until I found out it had to be entered in each man's record.

Our convoy consisted of five YMS's and one Landing Ship, Tank (LST) which was a fuel ship. We arrived in Uahuka and pulled into a harbor to refuel. The natives all ran when they spotted us. After one of our officers went ashore in the skiff and spoke to them in French, they all came out to trade. Well, we found out one thing. "Do not drink cocoa nut milk in any amount if you want to keep your shorts clean."

Our next port of call was Samoa. The island was beautiful. The natives were all friendly and spoke English. Here, we really got sucked in. This smiling Samolian came aboard with the good news that his family was giving us a welcome dinner with roast pig and dancing girls. The entire crew, including officers, really fell for it. Could we help? Yes, there were a few things in short supply due to the war. The next day he came back with his family to pick up a case of rice, a case of this, and a case of that. The party was to be the following evening so they would kill the pig that morning and start the roast. We were anxiously waiting when he appeared the next morning with the sad news, "Party is off. His brother was wounded by the pig and he was the only one who knew how to cook the pig."

Before we left for Bora Bora, we found out this was a game that had been pulled off many times by the natives. Of course, it was always at the expense of small ships. Bora Bora was also beautiful and you guessed it—no party. We were now getting radio transmissions from the combat zone. The Jap Fleet was moving down from up North.

We passed Guadalcanal which was completely under control by our forces and then headed for New Guinea where we picked up some supplies. I went over to the Army Supply Base for some office equipment and ran into Willie Mays, an old classmate. We had quite a visit. When I was getting ready to leave, he gave me a hunting knife which he said I would need when I got up North. I still have that knife and always wished I could find Willie to let him know I carried it daily.

While we were in New Guinea, we traded with the natives for bunches of green bananas. We hung them up in the rigging so they would ripen. We had been at sea for two weeks heading for Manus our next supply stop. The watches on the ship were four on and eight off. I had finished the eight to twelve o'clock watch on the flying bridge and came down into the galley. Sitting there drinking my coffee, I happened to look over at the doorway. I noticed what seemed like a wooly worm on top of the threshold. All of a sudden it went back. "Wooly worms don't back up." I was dumb-founded when I went over to see and find a very large tarantula spider outside on the deck. He had apparently come aboard with the bananas. I took a coffee can and put it over him. Then I flipped it over with a knife. He more than covered the bottom of the coffee can. That spider had been crawling around the ship for some time. After I showed the spider to the Captain the next day, the spider went overboard.

Manus was our next stop. The Jap planes made nightly visits. They blew up an ammunition ship while we were there. Luck was with us as we had anchored behind a hill and the blast went over the top of us. Our gunner's mate made contact with the munitions supply. With the trade of several cases of beer, we ended up with two more twin fifty's and two twin thirty's which really helped to gun us up. The rest of the YMS's called us the Midget Battle Ship.

After a few days here, we were ordered to a convoy bound for Leyte Harbor in the Philippine Islands. Our little peaceful excursion had come to an end. We were half way to Leyte one night when we received a radio transmission to break up and turn back as the Jap Fleet was coming down our way. All that night and for the next two days, we heard over the radio about the battle that was around us, but not within seeing distance. We spotted some of our planes, but no Japs. The third day we regrouped and headed for Leyte.

Leyte was swarming with our ships. It was quite a sight when the Jap planes came in. What a hell of a bunch of fireworks! The ack ack (anti aircraft fire) was so thick upstairs that you could walk on it. One day the Japanese forces moved an artillery piece up a hill looking over the harbor and started to fire a few rounds at the ships. We watched the South Dakota swing her guns around and the whole top of the hill went up in smoke.

We found out that we were regrouping for the invasion of Luzon. After a week at Leyte, we were ordered to leave that night for Luzon. We had about twenty ships in our convoy. Yard Mine Sweepers (YMS's), Auxiliary Mine Sweepers (AM's), one tanker, two four stack Destroyers (DD's) and one new DD for radar coverage. Our convoy was called Bus Boy.

Our convoy left Leyete late in the afternoon so that we would be in the Mindinero Straits by evening as the straits were still under Japanese control. Our convoy entered the widest part just at dusk. I was on the twenty mm and noticed a small plane approaching from the starboard. As it got closer, I could plainly see the red balls on its wings. I yelled for the bridge and opened fire with the old twenty. As soon as I fired, the convoy opened up. The little scout plane apparently made it back to base because the next morning just at day break, their welcome committee showed up with about fifteen Zekes. Luck was with us—no suicide pilots, just bombs and strafing. We really used up a bunch of ammo. Several Japs were knocked down, but no ships were sunk. Although our ship suffered no damage, the convoy had to have burial services.

After this, Japs kept hitting us day and night. We stayed at general quarters around the clock. I had a blanket handy to help me catch any sleep that I could. One night I awoke to the sound of gun fire. I was so groggy from the lack of sleep that I found myself trying to stuff the blanket instead of a magazine into the twenty. It was broadcast over and over from our lead destroyer. "Bus Boy! This is Porter. Bogies (Jap planes) at ten miles, closing fast." The third day we had just passed Corrigidor, which is the entrance to Manila Harbor, when Porter called, "Bus Boy! Bus Boy! Two Skunks twenty miles astern closing." We had never heard that term so out came the code book. Porter and the two old four stackers turned astern laying down a smoke screen as they went. One last radio message from Porter, "Disperse." Luck was with us again. Porter's second salvo hit the lead Jap destroyer so that both decided to run. Our convoy regrouped and we were on our way again.

The following day just before daybreak, we entered Linguyen Harbor. Here we experienced suicide planes for the first time. We were going along side of the Langley for some additional sweep gear when two Jap planes dropped down over the mountains. One picked out the Langley. In spite of intense fire from her and all the close ships, the plane hit the Langley in the wheel house. She was completely on fire as we watched the crew hit the water. The second plane took an AM sweeper, but it did not do much damage. The loss of crew was very high. We helped pick up survivors. This was very heart breaking to see the Langley burn and finally blow up. You didn't know whether to cuss or cry. Our convoy retired at sea that night.

We had been cruising for some time that night when disaster almost took us. The convoy sailed in a rather large circle so that we would be fairly close to Lingayen Gulf by daybreak. Danger came in the form of a large cruiser of our own fleet steaming at flank knots cutting right through our convoy. I was on deck when we heard this loud rushing sound and out of the night came this ship. It seemed as though we could have reached out and touched her as she went by. All of the convoy and this cruiser were running without lights and apparently she did not pick us up on her radar. Luck was with us again as no one was hit. Unfortunately, the Japs found us with flares. It was general quarters all night. We had the satisfaction of bringing down a Jap Betty (bomber) and several fighter planes.

We went back into Linguyen Gulf at daybreak. The fleet was supposed to be there to give us air coverage, but they were held up by Jap surface craft off Borneo. It was another bad day. Two more sweepers were sunk by planes. Every time we came close in sweeps to the shore we would come under mortar fire. The first time we came under fire, we thought it was a mine exploding. The second round just missed us. The ship went in a zigzag pattern to get the hell out of range. The following morning our fleet showed up along with an umbrella of Ack Ack. The Japs were really going after them. It was great to have some of the heat off us. We received a radio message from the fleet that they could not enter the harbor due to heavy air attacks.

That night, Tokyo Rose kept broadcasting about how the little sweeper would be annihilated the following day. The fleet moved in the next day accompanied by five battle wagons with several heavy cruisers and destroyers. The aircraft carriers stayed outside. Everything turned out better the next few days. We made one final sweep ahead of the landing craft and were almost taken by mortar fire from the beach. With the bombardment group firing over our heads, it was great to retire and get the hell out of there.

With Llnguyen Gulf completed, we headed for a landing at Subic Bay and then Corrigidor. This was another nervous operation because we were picked to go into Mariveles Harbor and the end of Battan to sweep the harbor. We swept so close to the shore that we came under sniper fire. I shot at everything that moved on the shore, including one old black and white cow. I never knew that it was a cow until it rolled out of the bushes.

We had a time getting by Corrigidor's guns. Our ship received the Navy Commendation Ribbon for this patrol. I received the letter and ribbon two years after the war was over.

The Air Force made a parachute landing on Corrigidor the next day and the poor paratroopers really got shot up before they hit the ground. Many of them landed on cliffs and some in the water. Manila Harbor became a turkey shoot after Corrigidor was secured. The Japanese army was retreating south. They were using anything that would float to cross the harbor. We tried to capture some of them. Instead they threw grenades at us so the only solution was shooting.

We came in the second morning and saw this sole Jap waving at us. He just had a small raft. Since the three inch had a real good telescope sight, we trained it at him. He knelt down at first expecting us to shoot and then he hollered "Detroit." He had no clothes on. We pulled up close to him and found out he was an American citizen who had been visiting relatives in Japan when the war broke out.

After Corrigidor was secured, we swept further into Manila Bay. One sweep carried us by the old concrete battleship with its old sixteen inch gun. I was looking it over through a pair of field glasses when I noticed a Jap was looking at us with glasses. The bay was full of retreating Japs and apparently some of them had holed up in this old deserted relic. The next day the Army tried to coax them out but finally had to blow them out with a gasoline bomb. On this sweep, we passed gun emplacements manned by Japs. It was nerve racking. The guns followed us as we passed, but did not fire. The harbor was full of sunken Jap ships that had to be cleaned out due to Japs trying to hide. At the same time the Army was going through Manila. The old Walled City gave them a rough time. It was here that the Japs killed some nuns.

On one of the islands, we pulled into the harbor to find the Japs had left. We swept for the Army so they could make a landing on the far side. Our intention was to cut off any of the enemy escaping. To our amazement, this island had a complete railroad system. It was a narrow gage track railway. All the engines and cars were parked. The skipper had us tie up to a dock and said part of the crew could go ashore. Gooch, our machinist mate, said, "I am an old engineer and I can fire these babies up." We soon had trains running everywhere. We even put two of the engines head to head for a tug of war. Tronaugh and I went over to the depot to look around and found all these tickets sequentially numbered. We had an idea so all the tickets went with us. By folding them over so the numbers were on the inside and sticking them on the desk pin, we had a real gambling game going. Prizes from one to five dollars would be given for certain numbers. Most of the several hundred tickets went in a hurry. The next day, Skipper said, "You two have enough of the ship's money so get rid of that." The army arrived the next day and took over our railway.

After Manila Bay we chased the Japs from one island to another. All action was minor as the Japs kept ahead of us. We were getting ready to head back for Leyte when the official word came down that we would join a group of sweepers headed for Tarakan Borneo. Tarakan Borneo was just off the mainland of Borneo. This was an island that you could sail around in a few hours.

We entered the first bay on the west side to sweep mines our planes had dropped months before. It was quite a surprise when the first mine exploded (acoustic mines set off by sound) and the whole harbor went up in smoke. Our next sweep was in the straight between the island and the mainland. We had noticed several shacks along the beach. We had been assured by the Aussie Air Force that almost all guns had been eliminated. We had made two passes into the straight and were making our turn to go out when the shacks all went tumbling down. There were the Japs and their guns only about 800 yards from us. We chopped our gear loose and tried to make a hasty exit; but we really got shot up. They did not make a good hit on us but blew the following sweeper out of the water. We lost our pet monkey and lots of rigging. We were lucky as the sweeper ahead of us took a shell in the wheel house. We had to go aboard her after we were out of the line of fire to help clean up and bury the dead.

After Tarakan we went up the coast to Milany Bay. We had a devil of a time sweeping submarine mines. They were anchored with chain instead of cable. Every time we brought in our gear, we had mines hanging in it. It was here that a mine exploded under us and I was thrown against the bulkhead. They took me over to a destroyer as we had only a pharmacist mate. The doctor said that I had probably broke something and advised that I turn into the hospital when we got back to Leyte. We broke down on the way back so we had quite a delay. By the time we got back to Leyte I was on my feet so I did not want to leave the ship.

We had been in the forward area over a year and were due for some relaxation and rest. While we were waiting, we heard the news that Hiroshima had been hit with an atom bomb. It was just a few days when we dropped the second bomb and the war was going to end. We were all excited about going home when we received orders to join the China Sweep Operation. We all really celebrated the end of the war when we got word that the Japanese government wanted to sign an unconditional surrender. All the flares went up in the night sky. All the beer came out.

The next morning it was business as usual. We were under way for Okinawa. When we left Leyte, we were informed that a typhoon was coming up from astern. It was several hundred miles from us so we thought we could make it to Okinawa. This turned out to be an error as the typhoon caught us when we were about halfway there. Our skipper had us well prepared with life lines all over the ship and hatches battened down. With our ship in top condition, we made it. It was quite an experience staying on deck, hanging on and being soaking wet for two days. We had swells up to ninety feet. This is what caused us to lose some of our sweepers. Calls for help just went unanswered as we were hanging on for dear life. Years after the war, I read in the report from the Mine Sweeper Association that our convoy lost ten vessels out of thirty.

Arriving in Okinawa was quite a sight. Ships were on the beaches, others rolled over, and the buildings had really been heavily damaged by the typhoon. Here we received our orders for Shanghai to sweep the Yangtze River and open up the port. The war was officially over. Yet we were warned to be on the lookout for Japs that were not willing to give up or had not heard the news.

We lucked out when we arrived at the Yangtze River and located the two magnetic mines our Air Force had dropped months before. We exploded them on the third pass. Our next sweep was the Huangpu River leading into Shanghai. No mines were found in this section of the river so we tied up in Shanghai that night. What a treat with neon lights ablaze and girls waiting on the dock. The Chinese were overjoyed with our arrival. Lots of the people here were white Russians. Liberty was the main event of the day. Out came the dress whites and we headed for town. Prices were cheap and American dollars were in heavy demand. Bars were plentiful and we were welcomed by everyone. We were all sitting in this one bar when McDonald came in with a Chinese girl. "I am going to get one thing settled," he said. He had the girl remove her pants to prove to us that Chinese girls were made the same as American girls. It did not seem to bother her one bit as long as she got the five bucks.

While we were in Shanghi, I met Victor Seaglove. His father had to flee Russia and was living there until they could relocate. Victor was about twelve and had a real good knowledge of the city. We rented a petty cab for the day and made rounds. Shanghai was a modern city in some ways and ancient in others.

Life in China had its cold reality. Victor took me by a cemetery. Since it was winter, all the corpses of people who had died were just wrapped and laid on top of the ground. You could see some of the bodies badly chewed up by animals. They would be buried in the spring. A rather violent event of quick justice happened as Victor and I were in the main business district. Shanghai uses Indian policemen. These Indians came from a certain tribe in that country. They wear turbans and are very large people. We were crossing the street when a loud commotion broke out with some screaming. A turban policeman came out of a store dragging this Chinese by the collar out in the middle of the street onto an island. He then put his pistol to the poor wrench's head and fired. He just calmly walked away from the poor dead man and continued directing traffic. When asked what happened, a bystander said, "He was a shoplifter." Our week visit passed quickly and then it was to the Chinese coast for more sweeping.

We made it back to Shanghai for New Year's. Prices had gone up as more service men arrived. Stevens, a deck hand, and I headed for town with two gallons of raisin jack that had just come out of the water kegs. It had been brewing for two weeks so it really had a punch. We decided to take it to the Volga Bar in the German Bund District and let the old bartender sample it. His reaction to it was "goot." Being New Year's, he told us to set it on the table and enjoy it.

There was a German girl that hung out at the bar. We called her Ulga of the Volga. Well, Ulga of the Volga filled herself up on raisin jack and ended up dancing on one of the tables minus most of her clothes. We let her name remain after that. They had a German band at the Volga. Dummy me. I suggested that they play God Bless America. The leader responded with, "You want what Patewy?"

We left Shanghai and headed down the coast to Amoy and Swatow. At Swatow we ran into the Communist Army. Part of our crew went on liberty in the town and found some firecrackers which they fired off in the town square. I was with McDonald and had just arrived when we heard the popping of fireworks. Almost immediately, some soldiers showed up and started knocking people down with their rifle butts. McDonald and I started to run when we saw they were headed for us. It was just a few blocks to the ship and we made it in no time. I saw that the soldiers were not stopping so McDonald and I uncovered the twenty mm and swung it around at them. It just took one short burst to convince them we were serious. The rest of the crew, including the officers, showed up when they heard the gunfire. Well, we untied and left that night.

Our next stop was Amoy, the pewter works of China. Here we had run out of fresh meat and decided along with another YMS to procure some. Our only choice was a water buffalo which was tied up on the dock. Our chief machinist mate, Lockman, decided to put the animal down with a sledge hammer. He took one mighty swing and hit the buffalo between the horns. The only results were the old buffalo shook his head and took a lunge at Lockman. Well it took a forty-five behind the ear to get our butchering job under way. We filled our freezer, the freezer on the other YMS, and gave the rest of the meat to the Chinese. The meat was a little tough but not bad to taste.

After finishing our sweeps, we headed for Hong Kong. There was no place like the entrance to Hong Kong, the city in the hills. We had some great liberties here. You could buy or see anything. The harbor was full of ships, a lot British. The harbor was also loaded with Junks. The Chinese live the year round on them.

From Hong Kong we headed for the Gulf of Tompkin. We had several sweepers with us. The minefield that we had to sweep was close to a group of dead volcanoes. They were about twenty miles from the mainland so we would anchor that night in a harbor between them. Trobaugh, Quinland, and I asked Skipper if we could take the skiff one day and stay on the shore for the day until the ship returned that afternoon. We took along some lunch and a 22 rifle, and went ashore on one of the volcanoes. There was an old lookout on the top of the mountain so we decided to climb up to it. Along the way, we spotted quite a few snakes and shot them with the 22. We had reached the top and were coming down when Trobaugh said, "Man did you guys see that big snake?" It had crawled into some bushes so we started to throw rocks into the brush. All at once the head of the snake reared up above the bushes. When its neck flattened out, we realized we were looking at a King Cobra. That snake must have been at least ten foot long. With no ammunition left for the rifle, we cleared out.

Our sweep of the minefield at this location was finished. Our next orders were for the entrance to Hinan River where our Air Force had dropped several magnetic mines during the war. We arrived at the harbor and were proceeding up the river when someone decided to give us a welcome with a burst of machine gun fire. It did not take our skipper long to retreat. I remember his words. "To hell with them. I hope they blow themselves out of the water."

It was now the last of January and we received word that the crew could be released as soon as replacement arrived. I had trained Higgins with my job. Therefore when we went back to Hong Kong, I told Captain Struve that I was leaving. I had been doing more deck work than my regular job because we were short of riggers for our sweeping. The Old Man asked me to stay for another month, but I was determined to head for home. I said goodbye to the crew and headed for the Port Director for transportation to the states. As I had been delayed so long after the war, he gave me top priority for air transportation to the United States. I remembered that bad experience I had with a plane in the Philippines when I flew to the Admiralty Islands for our mail. The plane, an old two engine C54, lost one engine. At that time, I had said, "Just let me make this one and I will never fly again." We threw everything that was not tied down out of that plane to keep it in the air. Therefore, I told the Port Director that I would wait for a ship. The ship arrived two weeks later. In the mean time, a boatswain mate and I spent every day down at the British Service Man's Club drinking warm beer. It's a wonder that I did not become a drunk.

The ship that arrived was a big troop transport with several thousand soldiers on board. I will never forget the smell down below decks. Vomit, smoke from a million cigars and cigarettes, and dirty socks and bodies formed that aroma. I went to the personnel office on top deck and volunteered for duty. I knew that I could expect a clean ward. The trip back was monotonous. We encountered one mine floating in the ocean miles from no where. You would have thought it was a pack of enemy subs the way they reacted. It took them an hour to sink it. They never could have made the sweep bunch.

Our first stop was Japan. We were told that the crew could have liberty for three days here. I took a train ride from the port to Tokyo. Upon coming back, I got on the wrong train and arrived in what was left of Hiroshima. It was an ungodly sight with just rubble as far as you could see. Off in the distance I could see the skeletal remains of some buildings. I had to take a bus back to our ship. At that time, I would not have felt so secure had I known anything about radiation.

Arriving in San Francisco, I was met by my brother George. All the hoopla of the war's end was gone. I was just another service man coming home. At least the Red Cross was at the dock with coffee and doughnuts. George and his wife, Phil, gave me a tour of San Francisco before I headed for Minneapolis for discharge.

While I was at the Minneapolis Discharge Center, everything was routine. I was just finishing up when the last doctor called me back and wanted to know why I was leaning slightly to the starboard. I told him about the mine explosion. He told me to report to the hospital. I knew I was discharged so I got on the train and headed for Sioux Falls, South Dakota.

Howard and Lillian met me at the depot and you would have thought I was a real hero. Everywhere we went, Howard would want me to show off my ribbons and tell a few war stories. Well I was a little hyper or at least did not have good control over my thoughts so it made it a little difficult. I just wanted to go home and see the folks. The following weekend, they took me home to Estelline.

Yard Mine Sweepers

LUZON EXPRESS, OUR BOMBARDMENT GROUP

Five battlewagons—Our help arrives.

- MAC ARTHUR'S COMMUNIQUE OF FEB. 17, 1945 -

MINESWEEPERS WERE SENT IN TO CLEAR THE AREA AROUND BATAAN AND
CORRIGADOR  X  GENERAL MAC ARTHUR CREDITS THIS OPERATION OF
THE MINESWEEPERS AS SKILLFUL AND DARING  X   AFTER THE MINE
SWEEPERS HAD CLEARED THE AREA IN FACE OF ENEMY FIRE CRUISERS
AND DESTROYERS FOLLOWED AND CARRIED OUT SHELLING OF GUNS AND
FORTIFICATIONS.

USS

YMS

363

# Where the fleet goes, we have been.

Capt. Struve with one of
two paintings I made.

My old twenty

I kept the record.

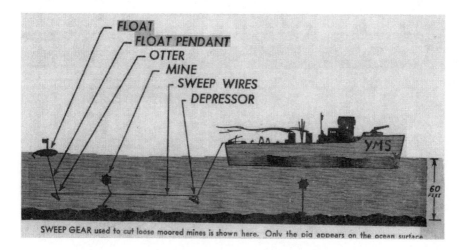

FLOAT
FLOAT PENDANT
OTTER
MINE
SWEEP WIRES
DEPRESSOR

YMS

60
FEET

SWEEP GEAR used to cut loose moored mines is shown here. Only the pig appears on the ocean surface.

# BEACHHEADS TO MANILA

SPEARHEAD for the assault on Luzon's beaches was the armed might of Vice Admiral Thomas C. Kinkaid's 7th Fleet. One of the battleships and a formation of destroyers that took part in the operation are pictured as they moved into Lingayen Gulf. These are the ships that laid down a blistering bombardment, the spade work for the beachhead.

*we had been looking for*

Official U. S. Navy photograph

*Luzon:* Our forces have landed on Luzon.

In a far-flung amphibious penetration our troops have seized four beachheads in Lingayen Gulf.

LUZON INVADED
IN BIG AMPHIB
OPERATION

The movement was covered by a blistering naval and air bombardment using both land-based and carrier-based planes. The enemy's air force made repeated and desperate attacks against our naval force formations in an endeavor to break the cohesion of our movement, but, beyond inflicting some loss and damage, was unsuccessful.

In these encounters there were destroyed 79 enemy planes, one midget submarine, two destroyers, one coastal cargo ship and many small harbor and coastal craft.

The enemy evidently had not prepared for a landing in the Lingayen sector and as a result of this strategic surprise, our landing losses were insignificant. We are now in his rear. His main reinforcement and supply lines to the Philippines are cut and his ground fight for Luzon will have to be made with such resources as he now possesses there. The back door is closed. The decisive battle for the liberation of the Philippines and control of the Southwest Pacific is at hand.

General MacArthur is in personal command at the front and landed with his assault troops. Ground forces of the 6th Army are under Gen. Walter Krueger. His naval forces of the 7th Fleet and an Australian squadron are now under Vice Admiral Thomas C. Kinkaid, USN, and his air forces of the Far East Air Force are under Lt. Gen. George C. Kenney. The 3d Fleet under Admiral William F. Halsey Jr., USN, is acting in coordinated support.

KANDY, Ceylon, *15th Indian Corps communique*—British troops and men of the Royal Indian Navy were engaged in brisk action with the enemy to the northeast of Akyab.

**10 JANUARY**

A record of landings made
and mines swept. We had
the record for YMS's

Leyte Harbor—waiting for another strike

# Office of the President
## of the Philippines

## P R O C L A M A T I O N

MY BELOVED PEOPLE:

The American forces of liberation under the brilliant leadership of General MacArthur have destroyed the enemy army defending Leyte, established control of Mindoro, and now stand firmly on the soil of Luzon within striking distance of our Capital City. This is the answer to our prayer of many long months. The decisive hour in the Battle of the Philippines has arrived.

General MacArthur has called upon us to rally behind him and I know that every patriot, guerrilla and civilian, will heed that call so that the enemy may feel the full strength of our outraged people. Rally to his forces with your utmost so that his burden of battle may be lightened. Rise to noble heights as a liberty-loving people. Acquit yourselves with courage and honor worthy of the sacred memory of our departed heroes.

God defend our cause! God strengthen our arms! God speed the day of our deliverance!

SERGIO OSMEÑA
President of the Philippines

Message on previous page:


MY BELOVED PEOPLE:

The American forces of liberation under brilliant leadership of General MacArthur have destroyed the enemy army defending Leyte, established control of Mindoro, and now stand firmly on the soil of Luzon within striking distance of our Capital City. This is the answer to our prayer of many long months. The decisive hour in the Battle of the Philippines has arrived.

General MacArthur has called upon us to rally behind him and I know that every patriot, guerrilla and civilian, will heed that call so that the enemy may feel the full strength of our outraged people. Rally to his forces with your utmost so that his burden of battle may be lightened. Rise to noble heights as a liberty-loving people. Acquit yourselves with courage and honor worthy of the sacred memory of our departed heroes.

God defend our cause! God strengthen our arms! God speed the day of our deliverance!


SERGIO OSMENA
President of the Philippines

## Manila Bay (13-19 February 1945)

The spotlight of invasion focused next on Manila Bay. From the beginning, it was expected that minesweepers would encounter heavy opposition from the shore batteries located at Manila and on nearby Corregidor and Caballo Islands. Cruisers and destroyers were assigned to this force to provide fire support for the sweepers and to conduct shore bombardment of enemy positions when and where they might be disclosed.

This powerful task group left Subic Bay on 13 February. Sweep operations commenced on the approach to Manila and continued on into the waters to seaward of Corregidor. Here the task group split up onto separate units, each having its own fire support stations when the sweepers commenced operations.

Shortly after noon on the following day shore batteries on Corregidor opened up on a YMS formation as it approached. Five hits were scored almost immediately on the guide sweeper which caught fire and had to be abandoned as she lay dead in the water without steering or engine control. A destroyer moving in to rescue personnel took a direct hit on the forecastle. All sweepers were ordered to clear the area and a second destroyer went to the assistance of the stricken YMS. Meanwhile, fleet units lying off shore poured a tremendous volume of fire into Corregidor. Planes were ordered up to lay a protective smoke screen under cover of which the destroyer rescued survivors of the YMS. As this vessel was drifting towards the enemy beach the destroyer was ordered to sink here, which she proceeded to do, at the same time taking the enemy guns on Corregidor under fire. The remaining sweepers managed to retire in order although one YMS was the target of several Jap salvos.

In the afternoon sweeps were made into Mariveles Harbor by YMS vessels. It was during this part of the operation that two destroyers were mined while following close astern of the sweeper formation to assist with mine disposal. This incident came as a complete surprise as the destroyers were proceeding very slowly in swept waters. It is believed that the mines must have been Japanese controlled mines. Other vessels were immediately dispatched to render assistance, but both destroyers were able to retire from the area under their own power.

On February 15th YMSs worked into Caballo Bay and swept one mine at the entrance. Shore batteries inside the bay opened up and a YMS took a hit in the generator room from a 3-inch armor peircing shell.

Only a few of the many sweep operations have been mentioned here. The names of the places where sweepers have streamed their gear make an impressive list - Leyte, Mindoro, Lingayen, Manila, Balabac, Palawan, Coron Bay, Albay Gulf, San Bernardino Strait, Ormoc Bay, Tawitawi, Zamboanga, and others. The majority of the sweepers took part in several of these operations, sometimes concluding one and setting off for the next without pausing any longer than was nexessary to fuel and porvision. Severe strain and fatigue were experienced by all personnel involved, and the tension was heightened by prolonged and determined air attacks in some areas and the raking fire of strongly entrenched shore batteries in others. The minesweeping forces acquitted themselves with distinction under most difficult and hazardous conditions.

Message on previous page:

## MANILA BAY (13-19 FEBRUARY 1945)

The spotlight of invasion focused next on Manila Bay. From the beginning, it was expected that minesweepers would encounter heavy opposition from the shore batteries located at Manila and on nearby Corregidor and Caballo Islands. Cruisers and destroyers were assigned to this force to provide fire support for the sweepers and to conduct shore bombardment of enemy positions when and where they might be disclosed.

This powerful task group left Subic Bay on 13 February. Sweep operations commenced on the approach to Manila and continued on into the waters to seaward of Corregidor. Here the task group split up into separate units, each having its own fire support stations when the sweepers commenced operations.

Shortly after noon on the following day shore batteries on Corregidor opened up on a YMS formation as it approached. Five hits were scored almost immediately on the guide sweeper which caught fire and had to be abandoned as she lay dead in the water without steering or engine control. A destroyer moving in to rescue personnel took a direct hit on the forecastle. All sweepers were ordered to clear the area and a second destroyer went to the assistance of the stricken YMS. Meanwhile, fleet units lying off shore poured a tremendous volume of fire into Corregidor. Planes were ordered up to lay a protective smoke screen under cover of which the destroyer rescued survivors of the YMS. As this vessel was drifting toward the enemy beach the destroyer was ordered to sink her, which she proceeded to do, at the same time taking the enemy guns on Corregidor under fire. The remaining sweepers managed to retire in order although one YMS was the target of several Jap salvos.

In the afternoon sweeps were made into Mariveles Harbor by YMS vessels. It was during this part of the operation that two destroyers were mined while following close astern of the sweeper formation to assist with mine disposal. This incident came as a complete surprise as the destroyers were proceeding very slowly in swept waters. It is believed that the mines must have been Japanese controlled mines. Other vessels were immediately dispatched to render assistance, but both destroyers were able to retire from the area on their own power.

On February 15th YMSs worked into Caballo Bay and swept one mine at the entrance. Shore batteries inside the bay opened up and a YMS took a hit in the generator room from a 3-inch armor piercing shell.

Only a few of the many sweep operations have been mentioned here. The names of the places where sweepers have streamed their gear make an impressive list—Leyte, Mindoro, Lingayen, Manila, Balabac, Palawan, Coron Bay, Albay Gulf, San Bernardino Strait, Ormoc Bay, Tawitawi, Zamboanga, and others. The majority of the sweepers took part in several of these operations, sometimes concluding one and setting off for the next without pausing any longer than was necessary to fuel and provision. Severe strain and fatigue were experienced by all personnel involved, and the tension was heightened by prolonged and determined air attacks in some areas and the raking fire of strongly entrenched shore batteries in others. The minesweeping forces acquitted themselves with distinction under most difficult and hazardous conditions.

# Corregidor and Manila

**BATAAN CAPTURED IN AMPHIB MOVEMENT FROM OLONGAPO**

**YANKS LAND ON CORREGIDOR ISLAND FROM SEA AND AIR**

OUR FIRST JAP FLAG

Lt. John Rex Hodges, USNR, captain of the *Salute*, reported that the mines were the standard Jap contact type and that they were popping up so fast it was almost impossible to hold formation. On the first day of the sweep, Jap 75-mm. batteries on both Corregidor and Carabao opened up on the fleet sweeps. A few of the shells from *Salute* landed within 25 yards of Corregidor so Lt. Parker A. Kitchell, USNR, (the gunnery officer, later exec) decided he'd had enough. He took charge of the three-inch gun and, with none of the modern fire-control devices used on larger ships to aid him, fired 150 rounds into the Corregidor emplacements. The Japs quit.

After Manila Bay, where one Min-Div also swept American moored control mines sowed before the Jap invasion in 1941, and similar-type enemy mines operated electrically from a control post on land, the *Salute* and other sweeps in the division continued their job of clearing up other waters off Philippines shores. They swept the east coast of Luzon in March, off Legaspi and through San Bernardino Strait in April and then headed for new waters—Balabac Straits betwee Palawan and Borneo.

ADVANCED HEADQUARTERS ON LUZON— We have landed on Corregidor and seized its decisive points. Its complete capture is now assured. With light casualties following bombardment by the 7th Fleet and the Far East Air Force, the 11th Corps, in a closely coordinated parachute and amphibious movement plished a double landing.
503d Parachute Regiment successfully dropped on the topside of Corregidor, taking its batteries and defenses in the war. Shortly thereafter elements of the 24th Division ferried across the narrow channel from Bataan and landed on Corregidor's south shore. They immediately advanced inland and joined the paratroopers. The recapture of Bataan and Corregidor clears the entrance to Manila Bay and opens this great harbor to our fleet.

**AMERICANS LAND ON CORREGIDOR FROM SEA, AIR**

Five miles of open water separates Corregidor from Carabao. Slowed by the four-knot drag of their heavy sweeping gear, the AMs started down the broad channel, "cutting mines like mad." When 78 had been gouged from the bay, the sweeps turned back and started the nasty job of detonation. Some skippers preferred rifle fire while others relied on 20s and even 40s to sink or explode them.

ADVANCED HEADQUARTERS ON LUZON— On Corregidor we are clearing out enemy pockets. Units of the 7th Fleet shelled the Cavite shore line south of Corregidor. Our navy units in the vicinity of Manila Bay sank five small enemy craft.

Painted by a PT Officer.

Para-troops
Rain down
Corregidor.
The first
waves softe

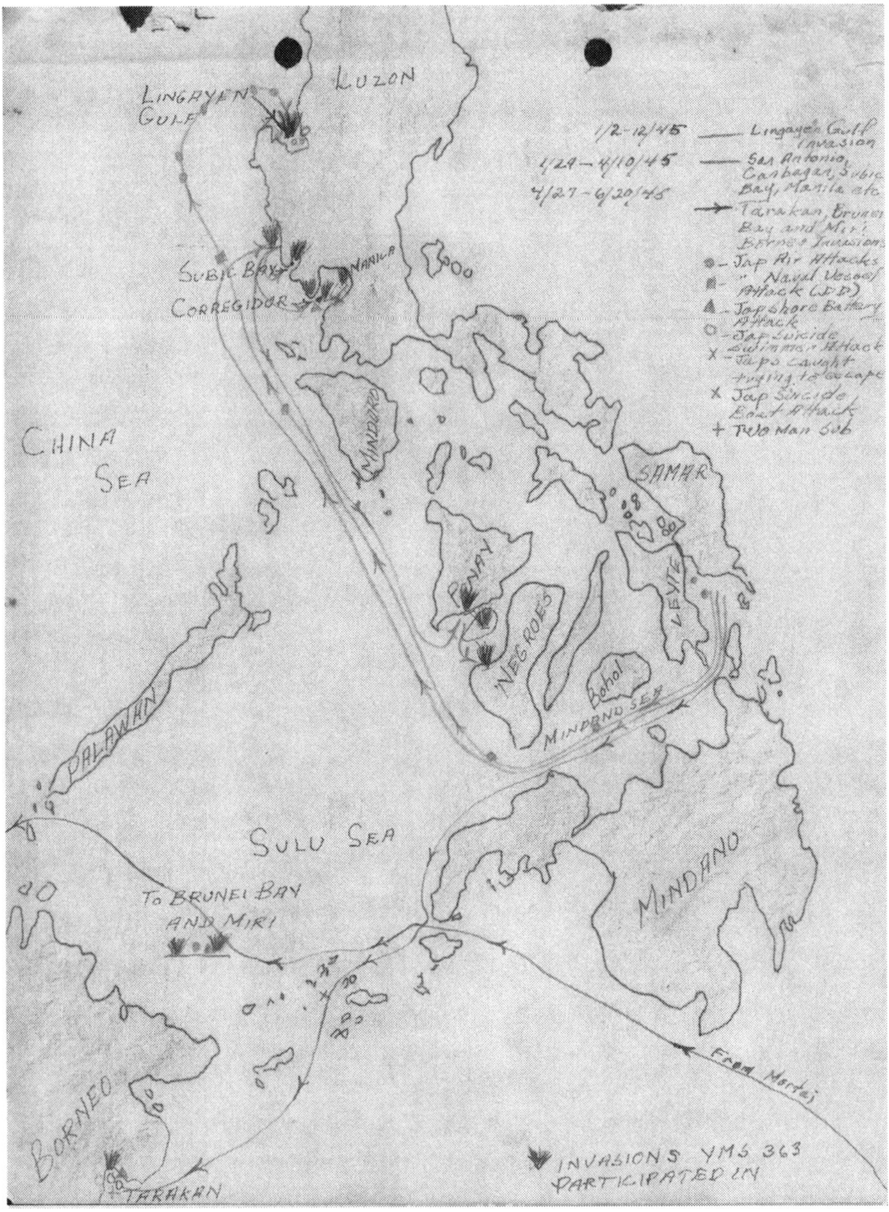

LINGAYEN GULF

LUZON

1/2-12/45 —— Lingayen Gulf Invasion
1/29-4/10/45 —— San Antonio, Cañabagan, Subic Bay, Manila etc.
4/27-6/20/45 → Tarakan, Brunei Bay and Miri, Borneo Invasions
● — Jap Air Attacks
▣ — " Naval Vessel Attack (D.D.)
▲ — Jap Shore Battery Attack
○ — Jap Suicide Submarine Attack
× — Japs caught trying to escape
✕ — Jap Suicide Boat Attack
+ — Two Man Sub

SUBIC BAY
CORREGIDOR
MANILA

CHINA SEA

MINDORO

SAMAR

PANAY

NEGROES

LEYTE

Bohol

PALAWAN

MINDANO SEA

SULU SEA

MINDANO

To BRUNEI BAY AND MIRI

From Morotai

BORNEO

TARAKAN

♦ INVASIONS YMS 363 PARTICIPATED IN

Official U. S. Navy photograph

SMOKE belches from a 7th Fleet heavyweight throwing knockout punches at the Jap defenses dug in on Luzon coast

Official U. S. Navy photograph

SALVO from a battleship's guns hangs out a wreath as shell are pumped into the Japanese shore defenses on Luzon

Official U. S. Coast Guard photograph

WALLOWING through the South China Sea, LSTs, boxcars of task force, brought up men and equipment for the push.

Official U. S. Coast Guard photograph

FIRST WAVES of Yank troops climbed down cargo nets into landing barges while the fleet was concluding its barrage.

Official U. S. Navy photograph

UMBRELLA of flak was put up when Jap bombers tried to get at the American invasion armada inside Lingayen Gulf.

. . . Plane plunges into sea between burning destroyer and a second DD to left of the splash . . .

. . . and disappears under cloud of smoke and steam as the undamaged destroyer pulls swiftly away.

AM 294

Lost at BRUNEI BAY, BORNEO

## The Last Pass

During the first two days of the operation the *Salute* and her sister ships cut about 40 mines, mostly across the main entrance to the bay where a fairly thick field had been laid. They could take no chances so they moved in on another pass, deep into the bay and out. *Salute* was guide ship, leading a wedge formation to speed the job. Not far from the bay entrance a tremendous explosion shook her and—men on other ships said—lifted her clear out of the water. She shuddered and settled, her crew rattling about the decks like ten-pins in a bowling alley.

When the smoke and spray had cleared they inspected the damage. A hole had been blown through her bottom and all decks up through the boat deck. Her back was broken. Nine men were dead, eight wounded. For seven hours she remained afloat, then she slipped quietly to the bottom, a year after she'd cleared her first minefield.

Two days later Australia's Diggers punched ashore seven miles from where the *Salute* lay in her watery but glorious grave.

DD WILLIAM D. PORTER goes down by stern while small rescue ship stands by. She sank three hours after attack.

At Lingayen Gulf, the *California's* gunners got the first Kamikaze and seemingly had the second one. She was hit and appeared to be skimming over the ship, doomed to hit the water harmlessly. But she banked suddenly, soared in upside down and crashed against a tower. The fires were extinguished in 12 minutes.

The *California* made temporary underway repairs and continued her assignments at Lingayen. Only when her chores had been completed did she head back for repair at Puget Sound.

Gunners of the *Newcomb* had out-shot numberless suicide pilots at Mindoro, Lingayen Gulf and at Okinawa on earlier occasions. But on 6 April off Ie Shima, seven Kamikazes attacked within two hours and, although three were shot down, four hit. The seventh got a double—it skidded across the literally disemboweled *Newcomb* and crashed head on into the stern of the uss *Leutze*, which had come alongside to help fight her fires.

A total of 175 casualties were suffered on the two DDs. Aboard the *Newcomb*, 17 were killed, 54 wounded and 20 missing. The *Leutze* had two killed, 68 wounded and 14 missing.

Only the heroic efforts of the *Newcomb's* crew—who fought with their hair aflame and their clothes burned off—kept the destroyer afloat and enabled the less-damaged *Leutze* to tow her to an advanced repair base.

*A YMS under attack from Jap shore batteries on Corregidor*

Manilla
Bay

YMS 48
was sun...

**CORREGIDOR INVASION** Feb. 16, 1945 was a spectacular operation. Paratroopers were dropped on plateau while PT boats picked up men wh Lieut. Dwight Shepler, USNR, painted

FROM:          USS PHOENIX

TO:            ALL MINE SWEEPERS

               WELL DONE

*After the battle in the strait*
*Tarakan, Borneo, YMS 481 was*

PLAIN

310015

UPON BEING RELIEVED OF COMMAND MINECRAFT PACIFIC FLEET I THANK YOU
ONE AND ALL FOR YOUR ABLE SUPPORT DURING THE PAST YEAR AND WISH
YOU ALL FORTUNE AND GOD SPEED X

ACTION TO:     THE VICTOR ONE ATTACK GROUP.
               THE VICTOR ONE ABLE ATTACK GROUP.
               THE VISAYAN ATTACK GROUP.

COMMANDER SEVENTH FLEET HAS RECEIVED THE FOLLOWING MESSAGE FROM CINCSWPA X

1.     "PERSONAL FOR ADMIRAL KINKAID X PLEASE ACCEPT FOR YOURSELF AND
EXTEND TO ALL OFFICERS AND MEN INVOLVED MY HEARTIEST COMMENDATION FOR THEIR
BRILLIANT EXECUTION OF THE VISAYAN CAMPAIGN X IT IS A MODEL OF WHAT A LIGHT BUT
AGGRESSIVE COMMAND CAN ACCOMPLISH IN RAPID EXPLOITATION MACARTHUR" X

2.     COMMANDER SEVENTH FLEET ADDS HIS CONGRATULATIONS FOR A JOB WELL
DONE X TF AND TG COMMANDERS PLEASE INSURE THE DISTRIBUTION OF THIS MESSAGE TO
ALL UNITS LARGE AND SMALL X KINKAID" X

MAILGRAM
U. S. NAVAL COMMUNICATION SERVICE

DELIVER THIS MAILGRAM TO COMMUNICATION SYSTEM
IMMEDIATELY UPON RECEIPT FOR DISTRIBUTION
AND HANDLING AS A REGULAR DISPATCH

| FROM: TG 78.1 | DATE: 16 June 1945 |
|---|---|

| TO: TG 78.1 | CLASSIFICATION RESTRICTED |
|---|---|

SPECIAL INSTRUCTIONS
If not encrypted by originator do not
transmit by radio without thorough
paraphrasing and encrypting.

RELEASE
00

160305

THE FOLLOWING MESSAGE WAS RECEIVED FROM LIEUTENANT GENERAL
MORSHEAD, GENERAL OFFICER COMMANDING FIRST AUSTRALIAN CORPS
X FOR REAR ADMIRAL ROYAL X ON THE EVE OF YOUR DEPARTURE I WISH
TO EXPRESS ADMIRATION AND APPRECIATION OF THE THOROUGH
EFFICIENT GALLANT AND SUCCESSFUL MANNER IN WHICH THE NAVAL
FORCE UNDER YOUR COMMAND CARRIED OUT ITS VITAL ROLE IN BOTH
OF THE BORNEO OPERATIONS X THANK YOU FOR ALL YOUR HELP AND
COOPERATION X OUR BEST WISHES FOR FURTHER SUCCESSES AND GOOD
LUCK TO YOU ALWAYS X END X PASS THIS MESSAGE TO YOUR OFFICERS
AND MEN X ROYAL

Authenticated _D. J. Keane Jr._

D. J. KEANE Jr.,
1st.,Lt. AUS

P.S.N.Y. 1-20-44 PM        U.S.S. SAUNTER

NAVAL DESPATCH
_____

I      WE DD'S ADMIRE SPLENDID PERFORMANCE AND GUTS OF
N
F      MINESWEEPERS X GOOD LUCK
O
R      FROM: DESTROYER SQUADRON 49
M
A      CONGRATULATIONS ON A GOOD JOB   X   SEE YOU IN TOKYO
T
I
O                    DATE: 160940 FEBRUARY 45
N
  FROM: YOUNG (DD580)
C
O        CTU 78.3.6
P
Y

---

FROM: CINCPOA           142304/579           AUGUST 1945
TO : ALPOA

CEASE OFFENSIVE OPERATIONS AGAINST JAPANESE FORCES X CONTINUE SEARCHES AND
PATROLS X MAINTAIN DEFENSIVE AND INTERNAL SECURITY MEASURES OF HIGHEST LEVEL
AND BEWARE OF TREACHERY OR LAST MOMENT ATTACKS BY ENEMY FORCES OR INDIVIDUALS

---

TO : ALPOA                 PLAIN

CINCPAC HAS RECEIVED THE FOLLOWING MESSAGE FROM CINCLANT: HEARTIEST CONGRATU-
LATIONS TO YOU AND THE OFFICERS AND MEN OF YOUR COMMAND ON YOUR DRAMATIC SUCCESS
CULMINATING ON THIS MEMORABLE DAY IN COMPLETE VICTORY X YOUR OPERATIONS IN THE
PACIFIC AGAINST OUR BITTER ENEMY WILL BE RECORDED AS THE MOST BRILLIANT IN HIS-
TORY X WE OF THE ATLANTIC SALUTE YOU

DELIVER THIS MAILGRAM TO COMMUNICATION SYSTEM
IMMEDIATELY UPON RECEIPT FOR DISTRIBUTION
AND HANDLING AS A REGULAR DISPATCH

| FROM:<br>    CTG 78.1<br>TO  :  TG 78.1 | DATE:<br>  11 June 1945 |
|---|---|
| INFORMATION<br>    GOC 9 AUST DIV<br>    AOC RAAF MOROTAI | CLASSIFICATION<br><br>PLAIN |
| SPECIAL INSTRUCTIONS<br>IF NOT ENCRYPTED BY ORIGINATOR DO NOT<br>TRANSMIT BY RADIO WITHOUT THROUGH<br>PARAPHRASING AND ENCRYPTING. | RELEASE<br><br>ØØ |

110626

THE FOLLOWING RECEIVED FROM GENERAL MACARTHUR AND PUBLISHED

TO ALL HANDS WITH MY CONGRATULATIONS "FOR GENERAL MORSHEAD

X ADMIRAL ROYAL X ADMIRAL BERKEY AND VICE AIR MARSHAL

BOSTOCK X THE EXECUTION OF THE BRUNEI BAY OPERATION HAS BEEN

FLAWLESS X PLEASE ACCEPT FOR YOURSELF AND CONVEY TO YOUR

OFFICERS AND MEN THE PRIDE AND GRATIFICATION I FEEL IN

SUCH A SPLENDID PERFORMANCE X SIGNED MACARTHUR"

Authenticated

W. E. RICHERT, Lt. USNR

QM L - A - ØØ815 - 17Ø8ØØ Ø815 GR 59

BT MY HEARTEST THANKS FOR THE SPLENDID PERFORMANCE OF A

DIFFICULT TASK X NEW SUBJECT X REQUEST ACTION REPORT

COVERING BRUNEI OPERATION BE SUBMITTED AS SOON AS POSSIBLE X

REPORT ON MIRI TO YMS 340 WHO WILL PASS TO ME X BEST OF

LUCK TO ALL AND WILL LOOK FORWARD TO SEEING YOU ALL AGAIN BT

COMMANDER MINE DIVISION THIRTY-FOUR
USS AM 2 9 9

# Citations and Commendations

*Citations + Commendation*

REPORT ON ELIGIBILITY FOR
PHILIPPINE LIBERATION RIBBON
AS OF __15 MAY 1945__

## U. S. S. Y. M. S. 3 6 3

1. DID SHIP PARTICIPATE IN LANDING AT LEYTE GULF, 17-20 OCT., 1944? NO
2. DID SHIP PARTICIPATE IN AN ENGAGEMENT AGAINST THE ENEMY? YES
   PLACE: In Convoy from Leyte to Lingayen Gulf(Continual Air Attacks).
   DATE: 2 January 1945 to 9 January 1945.

   PLACE: Operation at Lingayen Gulf
   DATE: 9 January to 12 January 1945.

   PLACE: Operation at San Antonio, Canbangan, and Subic Bay.
   DATE: 29 to 31 January 1945.

   PLACE: Operation at Bataan Penisula, Corregidor, and Manila Bay.
   DATE: 12 February 1945 to 2 March 1945.

   PLACE: Operation at Panay, Guimaras, and Negroes.
   DATE: 20 March 1945 to 10 April 1945.

   PLACE: Operation at Tarakan Island, Borneo.
   DATE: 27 April 1945 to 3 May 1945.

   PLACE: Bombardment from Shore Batteries, Tarakan Island, Borneo.
   DATE: 2 May 1945.
   PLACE: *Operation at Brunei Bay & Miri, Borneo.*

3. HAS SHIP BEEN IN PHILIPPINE WATERS FOR A PERIOD OF 30 DAYS OR MORE
   SINCE 17 OCT. 1944: YES.
   DURING WHAT PERIOD? From December 29, 1944 to May 15, 1945.

---

ALPOA 23          201956 OCTOBER PLAIN PRIORITY

IT IS WITH GREAT PRIDE THAT CINCPOA TRANSMITS THE FOLLOWING MESSAGE FROM OUR
COMMANDER IN CHIEF PRESIDENT ROOSEVELT QUOTE X PERSONAL FROM THE PRESIDENT X
THE COUNTRY HAS FOLLOWED WITH PRIDE THE MAGNIFICENT SWEEP OF YOUR FLEET IN

ENEMY WATERS X IN ADDITION TO THE GALLANT FIGHTING OF YOUR FLYERS X WE APPRECIATE
THE ENDURANCE AND SUPER SEAMANSHIP OF YOUR FORCES YOUR FINE COOPERATION WITH
GENERAL MACARTHUR FURNISHES ANOTHER EXAMPLE OF TEAMWORK AND THE EFFECTIVE AND

INTELLIGENT USE OF ALL WEAPONS X TO THE OFFICERS AND MEN OF ALL SERVICES WHO
HAVE CARRIED THE FIGHT TO THE ENEMY AND TO THOSE WHO HAVE PLANNED AND HAVE
SUPPLIED THE NEEDS OF THE FIGHTING FORCES THROUGH THE YEARS IS DUE THE CREDIT

FOR THE SITUATION WHICH PROMPTED THE COMMANDER IN CHIEF OF THE ARMY AND NAVY
TO SEND HIS MESSAGE X TO ALL THOSE OFFICERS AND MEN QUOTE WELL DONE UNQUOTE X

HERBERT A. JOHNSON

*To you who answered the call of your country and served in its Armed Forces to bring about the total defeat of the enemy, I extend the heartfelt thanks of a grateful Nation. As one of the Nation's finest, you undertook the most severe task one can be called upon to perform. Because you demonstrated the fortitude, resourcefulness and calm judgment necessary to carry out that task, we now look to you for leadership and example in further exalting our country in peace.*

*Harry Truman*

THE WHITE HOUSE

28 February, 1946

Mr. Henry E. Johnson
Goodwin, S. Dak.

Dear Mr. Johnson:

It is a pleasure to write you upon your son's discharge from the Navy. The happy reunion that you both have anticipated is now a reality.

The magnificent sacrifices that you have made, as have millions of other persons, were necessary and unavoidable, but by no means have they been in vain. They have contributed immeasurably to the winning of the war.

In order that your son may resume his normal place as a vital member of his family, Church and community, I am sure he will be most grateful for the understanding which only you can give him in adjusting his thoughts and actions from war to peace. If, perchance, he needs assistance in this transition period, please remember that civilian agencies are provided for the express purpose of assisting discharged servicemen, and encourage him to contact the proper agency.

By his bravery and loyalty, he has earned the right to expect success and happiness in all his undertakings, and it is my sincere prayer and hope that he will be successful and happy in his future life.

Sincerely yours,

By direction of the
Commanding Officer

HERMAN E. SODERBERG
Chaplain, USNR

# NATIONAL WAR FUND
## South Dakota Committee

STATE HEADQUARTERS
PHONE 2595

MADISON, SOUTH DAKOTA

May 10, 1945

**Honorary Chairman**
GOV. M. Q. SHARPE

**State Chairman**
V. A. LOWRY
Madison

**Vice Chairman**
FRANK GUHIN
Aberdeen

**Treasurer**
ALBERT M. PARKER
Madison

**Campaign Director**
R. S. WALLACE
Madison

**Publicity Committee**
J. F. STAHL, Chairman
Madison
FRED C. CHRISTOPHERSON
Sioux Falls
HENRY J. SCHMITT
Aberdeen
R. W. HITCHCOCK
Rapid City
ROBERT D. LUSK
Huron
CHAS. H. J. MITCHELL
Brookings
L. W. ROBINSON
Mitchell
MORTON HENKIN
Sioux Falls

**District Chairmen**
1. C. S. BALL
   Vermillion
2. W. H. T. FOSTER
   Sioux Falls
3. VERN G. WOHLHETER
   Watertown
4. FRED D. SHANDORF
   Mitchell
5. WILLIAM RIBNICK
   Aberdeen
6. PAUL NOREN
   Pierre
7. HENRY A. BAUER
   Rapid City
8. GEORGE F. BAGGALEY
   Deadwood
9. RAY A. STRATTON
   Huron
10. G. T. MICKELSON
    Selby
11. J. F. LUNN
    Winner
12. L. B. BOORMAN
    Lennon

Herbert Alden Johnson
Y 2/c, USNR
USS YMS 363
% Fleet Post Office
San Francisco, California

Dear Mr. Johnson:

This letter will serve to acknowledge receipt of your
money order for five dollars to purchase an appropriate
remembrance for your mother on Mother's Day. Your
original letter was directed to the USO at Watertown,
South Dakota. Since the USO unit at Watertown has been
closed, the letter was forwarded to the USO at Sioux
Falls. The Director at Sioux Falls was not acquainted
with anyone in Watertown, and as I am the State Chairman of the USO, he sent it on to me asking if I would
see that your request was taken care of.

Judge Vern G. Wohlheter is our District Chairman at
Watertown. I sent the money order and your card to him
and asked him to see that your request was carried out.
I am sure that it will be, and that your mother will
receive your remembrance next Sunday.

Yours very truly,

V. A. Lowry
State Chairman

VAL:ap

## MINESWEEPING DUTY

This duty aboard a minesweeper,
Tis' the worst under the sun.
But it comes before every invasion,
As the first work to be done.

The credit that goes to the big ships,
Sometimes makes us fellows burn.
They forget the sweepers go in ahead,
And not always do all return.

When this war is over,
Then to the folks I will tell,
Of passes through enemy waters;
Through barrages of shot and shell.

Of the suicide planes ramming in;
The mines earthquaking blast;
It will all be memories then,
Just experiences of the past.

And when I go up to heaven,
Old St. Peter I will tell,
"I've had duty on a sweeper, Sir,
And have served my term in hell.

Sending you a little poem I stirred up.
                                    Herb.

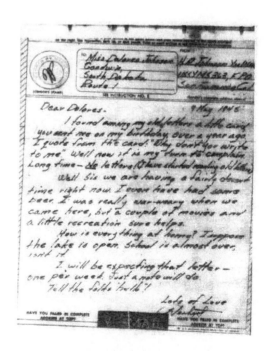

In reply address not the signer of this letter, but Bureau of Naval Personnel, Navy Department, Washington 25, D.C.

Refer to No.

'Pers-10

MM/648 09 67

4 NOV 1948

NAVY DEPARTMENT
BUREAU OF NAVAL PERSONNEL
WASHINGTON 25, D.C.

From:        The Chief of Naval Personnel.

'To :

            Mr. Herbert A. Johnson,                    bcd
            Goodwin, South Dakota.


Subject:     Navy Unit Commendation awarded TASK UNIT
             SEVENTY EIGHT POINT THREE POINT SIX.

Enclosure:   (A) Navy Unit Commendation Ribbon Bar.

1.    The Secretary of the Navy has awarded the Navy Unit
Commendation to the TASK UNIT SEVENTY EIGHT POINT THREE POINT
SIX for outstanding heroism in action against enemy Japanese
forces in the Manila Bay Area from February 14 to 18, 1945.

2.    By virtue of your service in the TASK UNIT SEVENTY EIGHT
POINT THREE POINT SIX during the period for which cited, you
are hereby authorized to wear as part of your uniform the
appropriate Navy Unit Commendation insignia.

                                    J.L. YOUNG
                                    By direction.

R-5064

March 20, 1946

My dear Mr. Johnson:

     I have addressed this letter to reach you after all the formalities of your separation from active service are completed. I have done so because, without formality but as clearly as I know how to say it, I want the Navy's pride in you, which it is my privilege to express, to reach into your civil life and to remain with you always.

     You have served in the greatest Navy in the world.

     It crushed two enemy fleets at once, receiving their surrenders only four months apart.

     It brought our land-based airpower within bombing range of the enemy, and set our ground armies on the beachheads of final victory.

     It performed the multitude of tasks necessary to support these military operations.

     No other Navy at any time has done so much. For your part in these achievements you deserve to be proud as long as you live. The Nation which you served at a time of crisis will remember you with gratitude.

     The best wishes of the Navy go with you into civilian life. Good luck!

     Sincerely yours,

     James Forrestal

Mr. Herbert Alden Johnson
R.F.D.
Goodwin, South Dakota

Shanghai 1945

(Revised August 1942)

Name __JOHNSON, Herbert Alden__

(Name in full, surname to the left)

__648 09 67__ rate __Y2c__ __V6__ __USNR__
(Service number)                        (USNR Class)

Date reported aboard __30 August 1944__

__U. S. S. Y. M. S. 3 6 3__
(Present ship or station)

__ARMED GUARD CENTER, NOLa.__
B A T T L E  (Ship or station)  R E C O R D

2 Jan. 1945: Under continual Air Attack by
enemy planes, while enroute from Leyte to
Lingayen Gulf, Philippines.

9-12 Jan. 1945: Participated in Minesweeping
and Landings at Lingayen Gulf, Philippines.

29-31 Jan. 1945: Participated in Minesweeping
and Landings at San Antonio, Cabangan, and
SubiC Bay, Philippines.

12 Feb. to 2 March 1945: Participated in Mine
sweeping and Landings at Baatan Peninsula
Corregidor and Manila Bay, Philippines.

14 Feb. Participated in Mineseeping Pass made
into Mariveles Harbor, Baatan Peninsula, P.I.

20 Mar to 10 Apr. 1945: Participated in Minesweeping and Landings at Panay, Guimaras,
and Negroes, Philippine Islands.

27 Apr. to 3 May 1945: Participated in Minesweeping and Landings at Tarakan, Borneo.

2 May 1945: Participated in engagement with
enemy shore batteries this date.

8-14 June 1945: Participated in Minesweeping
and Landings at Brueni Bay and Miri, Borneo.

To _____

__F. A. STRUVE, JR., Lt., USNR__
Signature and rank of Commanding Officer.

Date received aboard _____

_____
(New ship or station)

_____
(Last ship or station)

_____
Signature and rank of Commanding Officer.

ORIGINAL

FOR SERVICE RECORD        16—30510-1

(Revised August 1942)

Name  JOHNSON, Herbert Alden
<br>(Name in full, surname to the left)

648 09 67 rate Y2c, V6 USNR
<br>(Service number)          (USNR Class)

Date reported aboard  30 August 1944

U. S. S. Y. M. S.  3 6 3
<br>(Present ship or station)

ARMED GUARD CENTER, New Orleans, La.
<br>(Ship or station received from)

14 - 31 Sept. 1945: Participated in Mine-sweeping operations in Yangtze River Area, China.

20 Oct. to 11 Nov. 1945: Participated in Minesweeping in the HAIPHONG AREA, French Indo-China.

8 Sept. to 13 Dec. 1945: Participated in Minesweeping Operations in SWATO AREA, China

15 Dec. to 19 Dec. 1945: Participated in Minesweeping Operations in AMOY AREA, China.

20 Dec. 1945: Authorized to wear the World War II VICTORY RIBBON. Auth: ALNAV 352-45

Date transferred

To

J. J. DYKSTRA, Lt. (jg), USNR
<br>Signature and rank of Commanding Officer.

Date received aboard

(New ship or station)

(Last ship or station)

Signature and rank of Commanding Officer.

DUPLICATE

# Honorable Discharge

from the Armed Forces of the United States of America

*This is to certify that*

HERBERT ALDEN JOHNSON    YEOMAN T SECOND CLASS    V-6 USNR

*was Honorably Discharged from the*

# United States Navy

*on the* 30th *day of* APRIL 1952    *This certificate is awarded as a testimonial of Honest and Faithful Service*

M. E. D. YLE

LTJG USN

DD 259-N (REV. 5-50)

# CHAPTER 5

## Back Home

## 1946—1947

It really felt good to see Mom and Dad. For the first time in a couple of years, I got my feelings off my chest. It was so hard to finally believe I was out of danger with no more missions, no more heavy explosions, and no more waiting for something to happen. It was many months or even years before I could watch a sunset and not expect ack ack to start breaking. I know now that every combat veteran goes through the same thing. I was lucky to have Mom and Pop to talk to. I received a letter from Higgins telling me that I had been moved up to Yeoman 1st class.

Pop soon had me involved in the farm. First I went to the livestock sale to see what was selling. I spotted forty head of ewes and told Dad that I would really like to buy them. He just said go ahead and buy them and then go see Johnson at the bank. The next day I met Mr. Johnson, manager of the Estelline Bank. It was just a matter of signing a contract and the sheep were mine. Our next adventure was potatoes. Dad had some real good land for growing them. With another loan from the bank we had enough money for a potato planter, digger, and seed. Pop decided that day to plant by the light or dark of the moon. I don't remember which. His decision was sure the right one.

That summer was good to us and the potato crop. Rain came just at the right time and those potatoes really grew. We knew we were ahead of the big growers. Much to our delight, the time to harvest was a good two weeks ahead of any other growers. Pop and I attended an auction and found an old potato digger that, with a few repairs, was ready for the big dig. I went to Watertown and bought sacks. Then I went to Estelline for teenage help.

Everything worked out well. In a short time, we had the shed and barn full of sacked potatoes. Pop stored the small culls in another shed for future use. We were happy to find the going price at that time was $3.00 per sack. There was a local demand for the spuds, but not in any large quantity with a few sacks here and there. I finally went out to the highway and put up a sign, "Potatoes For Sale." Two nights later at about two in the morning a big truck towing a trailer pulled into the yard. We finally got dressed and to the door in time to hear, "I would like to buy some spuds." When he said two or three hundred sacks, you could have lifted Pop and me off the floor. We finally had him loaded and he reached into his pocket and paid in cash. We were in business! The last of the potatoes went fast.

Dad made his farm payment and had some left over so I decided to go deer hunting with Harry Jennings and Claude Chapman whom I had just met. They had both hunted in the Black Hills for years and had a real super place to stay. I was glad to get out of town just then. I had gotten involved with a red head and I did not want to hear wedding bells forced upon me. The three of us went to Iron Lake at an old CCC cabin with a huge fireplace. What a spot. There was enough room for a platoon. I shot a small forked horn the second day much to my disappointment. It was just a poor deer. Claude's neighbor came for the first weekend and did not have any luck so I gave him my deer. My thoughts were that then I would get a good one.

Claude was a fantastic shot for his age, 68. One day we came in from hunting when Harry's son and buddy came into the camp. His buddy was complaining that his new rifle was poorly sighted. Claude asked to see the gun and then skidded a brick way out on the lake until it was just a speck. Raising the gun up with no rest, he fired. Well that brick just turned into a red cloud of dust. He handed that rifle back and said, "'pears to me that gun sight's alright."

Well I hunted every day with no luck. Oh, I saw several bucks. One time I could not get my mittens off. Another, the buck was standing behind a very small tree which deflected the bullet. Yet another time, I had oiled the bolt to my rifle the night before and the cold weather caused the gun not to fire. The last day of the season arrived and I still had no deer. That last morning, I headed back to an area that both Claude and Harry had said to stay out of because I had to lower myself down on a rope for about thirty feet. Also it was a very stiff climb out of the other side. There was no way to take a deer out. Harry had told me earlier that he thought there was a road about fifteen miles to the south. I hunted all morning and into the afternoon. I sat down on a log to eat my last sandwich when a doe appeared.

Hoping that a buck might be following, I sat still. The doe was pawing off the snow for grass when out of the brush stepped the biggest buck I had ever seen. I had borrowed Claude's thirty-thirty which was easier to pack. My first shot knocked the buck down. The second went through his neck and that buck was mine. I gutted the buck out; but even then I could not drag him. I had the big hunting knife that Willie had given me while I was in the service. With this, I cut down two poles, used the rope I carried and made up an Indian skid. Getting in between the poles with the buck tied on, I headed south for the road. There was no moon. With the snow on the ground I had no trouble seeing where I was going. I hit that road at 2:30 in the morning and sat on my frozen buck wondering what to do. It was no more than an hour when a pickup came along. The driver's first words were, "Are you Johnson? The whole county is looking for you." I arrived back in Estelline as the great hunter.

While we were deer hunting, Harry Jennings talked me into trying my luck at selling tombstones. He was the district sales manager for Ortonville Monument Works. With a sales kit and no experience, I took to the road. It was a very cold and snowy winter when I was trying to get my start. In the next two months, I made one sale. This was for my Uncle Alfred who had passed away several months prior. It was just a matter of writing up the sale with Aunt Dora.

I was driving through Sioux Falls one cold day when I needed something at Johnson's Hardware Store. That store was the warmest spot I had been in since leaving home. With a small hope that I might have a chance for a job, I asked to see the owner, Warren Johnson. Mr. Johnson informed me that he had a full crew. Not wanting to give up, I suggested to him that he give me a try with the agreement that if he was not satisfied with my sales at the end of the week, he did not owe me anything. "Boy, you are desperate aren't you?" "Yes I am and damn sick of the cold weather." "You come to work in the morning," he said. "I just have to give you a try for a week." Well with the weather getting worse day by day, this was a real challenge for me. I sold and sold. By the week's end, my sales totaled almost four thousand dollars. This was more than double the totals of any other sales person in the store. I was hired permanently.

I enjoyed working at the hardware store. However, I had lost my love for South Dakota weather. I was looking forward to moving out west. Brother George came home for a visit. He had just bought an ice cream store in San Jose and wanted to know if I was interested in helping him and Phyllis, his wife, with the shop. I finished working at the hardware store and moved back with the folks in Estelline. Dad was not pleased to hear my new plans since he had planned that I would help him farm. My 1940 Chevrolet that I bought while in the service had to be worked over. Dad used it as a farm car while I was gone. It needed some attention.

# CHAPTER 6

## Going Out West
## 1947—1950

The day arrived when everything was ready to head west. My little brother, Leonard, asked to go along. Needing some company, I said yes. We took the trip through Washington, Oregon, and then California. I will never forget Leonard trying to hear the Lone Ranger on the car radio which was rather weak. He would be practically under the dash. In Washington, we stopped at the Strande Ranch where I spent my time in 1939. We went on to Yakima to see my Uncle Elmer. Then we headed down to Oregon where we crossed the Columbia River on a one car ferry. Finally, we ended up in San Jose, California.

Leonard went home on the bus while I went to work making ice cream and remodeling the store. We decided to add more to the store because we could use the empty room adjoining it. A salesman came by one day with a new hot dog machine. It could cook hot dogs in the bun in five seconds. This was just the item we were looking for. The machine cooked using an induction coil which we knew very little about, except that it worked. One day I was putting up fluorescent lights and George turned on the hot dog cooker. To our amazement, all the fluorescent tubes in the boxes lit up. With this knowledge in our belts, we decided to promote it. One of us would hold up two tubes in front of our customers and the other would hit the machine. Boy, what attention we got. It's a wonder that either one of us was ever able to conceive a live sperm with all that radiation.

My life was about to change because I met Marnie, Phil's sister. We were not really attracted to each other at first due to a date arranged by George and Phil. The following weekend I asked Marnie to go fishing at the coast.

That did it. I was in love. I had found a gal who was loving, sexy, and a hell of a pal. Marnie joined me in the love and enjoyment of the outdoors. We had a lot in common. A couple of months later, I hawked my Japanese rifle for a down payment on an engagement ring.

The ice cream store was not working for me so George and I decided to split up. I had a little Nash Rambler. I packed it and journeyed up to San Francisco where Marnie lived. My goal was to find a job there. I sent several cards out to hardware stores in the city and received an answer from Norman Hardware Store asking for an interview. I met Mr. Norman, an old cantankerous Swede with very poor vision. After listening to me, he said, "Johnson, you are Swede. You come and work for me." I replied, "O. K. Mr. Norman; but I want to take ten minutes off in the morning and afternoon for coffee." Mr. Norman replied, "No. We don't allow that here." "O. K. Mr. Norman. I don't want to work for you." Then I started out the door. I almost got to the door when he asked, "Did you say just ten minutes?" "That's right Mr. Norman." Well, he timed me for six months. I found that Mr. Norman, with all his ways, had a weakness. If he could not walk on you, he admired you. I was the only employee out of five that took time for coffee.

It was here that Marnie and I met Evelyn and Hobe Webb. They were the best of friends. We so enjoyed their company. Hobe and Evelyn were originally from South Dakota. Hobe was a practical joker and we had a lot of laughs together. One day the four of us went down to the Chinese District. Evelyn and Marnie were shopping when they complained that the clerks were constantly following them. We found out later that Hobe had told the clerks to keep a watch on the two women because they had a habit of shoplifting.

Another time on my day off, I was doing some work on our car in the basement. I had all my tools laid out and then decided to take the elevator up to the apartment for a cup of coffee. I shared the basement with the hardware store. When I came back down, I found all my tools gone. I was pure frantic. I questioned everybody and put notes in the elevator and hallways. I decided to go to the hardware store to see if any of the clerks had seen anyone. There were my tools all laid out on a counter with a sale sign. Old Hobe had struck again.

Marnie

# CHAPTER 7

## A New Life

## 1948—1960

Marnie and I set April 10, 1948 for our wedding. We found a studio apartment above the Norman Hardware Store. The wedding was planned between the two of us. I had to join the Catholic Church before the wedding date so I started a series of instructions. The day before the wedding, I finished with baptism, confession, and communion. During my first communion, I knelt at the railing with my arms on the railing. Then Marnie whispered, "Herb, they don't serve lunch here."

Well, our wedding day went off without a hitch. We traveled to Silverton, Oregon on our honeymoon. My brother Chuck and his wife Faith lived there. Brother Bob and his wife Mary Lou had recently moved there also, so we had a very good visit. Marnie and I were on our way home within a few miles from the Golden Gate Bridge when we discovered we had only twenty-five cents left. The toll on the bridge was fifty cents. We drove fifty miles out of our way to come in on the Bay Bridge which cost just twenty-five cents.

We loved our little apartment with the pull down bed. It was small with just a living room, a small bath and a very compact kitchen. We enjoyed it and even had overnight guests a couple of times. That really took some planning. I built a flower box to put out on the fire escape. What a time we had driving around San Francisco looking for dirt to fill it up. Life was good though. San Francisco was an interesting town and it was easy to meet people. Then the day arrived. Marnie was pregnant. How the two of us were excited. Not having a lot of room did not make any difference. We just wanted a baby.

While living in our little apartment over Norman's Hardware, we met Julie and Ken Spangler. Ken played football with the Petaluma Leghorns football team. We attended many of the games and became well acquainted with the football team. One of the players owned a thirty foot cabin cruiser and invited some of the players for a day bass fishing trip out on the bay. As there was lots of room, he asked me to go along. If I had known what was in store, I am sure I would have declined. Out on the bay, everyone was more interested in drinking beer than fishing. We started back late in the afternoon. We were about five miles from the dock and it was getting dark when our lights went out. The skipper said, "One of you go out on the bow and watch that we do not hit any floating debris. I will slow way down." I volunteered. To get to the bow, one had to walk along a narrow cat walk with the aid of a handrail. I reached out in the darkness to get hold of the handrail mistakenly grabbed the boat hook which was not supposed to be there. The next thing I realized I was off the boat and deep in the bay water. I came to the surface in time to see the boat disappear in the darkness. It is impossible to describe my feeling. I found my whole body frozen. It came to me all at once. "Herb, you have to try and loosen up or you are going to drown." I still had on my cap and was wearing a tight jacket and boots. The boots were my biggest handicap. In trying to unlace them, I sank too deep and could not hold my breath long enough. The Good Lord was with me for as I hollered as loud as I could, one of the fellows on the boat came out on deck. He told the skipper, "Herb's overboard and way back." The skipper shut off the engines without thinking. Then he could not restart it because the batteries were low. I started to swim toward the boat which was a good many yards away. The crew on the boat threw life rings, but they were way short. In the darkness, I would not have seen them anyway. If I had not had the boots and that tight jacket on, it would not have been such a problem. I made that boat with just a prayer. I was wet, weary and completely played out, but on board. To this day, I never go on a boat wearing shoes that I cannot slip off. I also keep a life jacket on or in hand.

About this time, more exciting news came. We had talked about having our own hardware store and the opportunity arrived. Mr. Norman's son, Jack, several years before had purchased a large amount of kitchenware for the store without the approval of his father. One thing that Mr. Norman did not care for was housewares. This one morning he approached me. "Johnson. Why don't you buy these housewares and start your own store? I will give you a price and credit to get started." "What kind of a price?" "Five hundred dollars." I knew that was one hell of a buy so I agreed. That night

Marnie and I went down to the store and started packing up the goods. We inventoried them at the same time. We found we had over twenty-five hundred dollars in good housewares. Now, where to put them?

Our friend Hobe came to the rescue. "I have a big basement garage that you can use." Marnie and I started moving the housewares over to Hobe's garage. We discovered that Hobe had a bigger garage than we expected. Norman Hardware always had a lot of shipping and packing material in their garbage. It was everything from lumber to paneling, etc. With this in mind, I started to salvage any usable items that I could make store counters of. Along with some paneling I bought, Hobe's basement was soon full of counters. Although Marnie was expecting, she still worked with me every night. I can still remember Hobe hollering down the stairs, "You had better get that woman out of there or that baby is going to be born in the basement."

Time came for Marnie to deliver. Our first baby was born in a Catholic hospital in San Francisco, not in Hobe's basement. We named him Gregory Allen Johnson and were quite proud. After his delivery, I went across the street to a little restaurant for a cup of coffee. I told the waitress that I was now a father. Dog gone it. She was not even impressed. We had a baby bed all ready for Greg in our little studio apartment. He was a very good baby with only one problem. When he was on his back while being changed, we discovered he could hit the shelf above the bed. What pressure that kid had.

The time arrived that we had to "S" or get off the pot. Hobe's basement was full of our counters and merchandise. We looked across the bay in Oakland for a store location. After a few days of scouting, we found a little building next to a grocery store with a small apartment behind. The landlord, Jack Kohn, was real nice and thought we were doing the right thing. He had been in business all his life.

It was with high hopes that we said good-bye to Mr. Norman and headed across the bay. We took our counters, merchandise, five hundred dollars in cash, and five hundred dollars in credit to start our new life. We received our business license and arranged our little store. After obtaining our sign, "Herb's Little Hardware Store," we opened for business. What an excitement the first night after closing when we counted up our day's receipts. We were in business!

Marnie and I kept our little store going for over a year when Jack Kohn approached us with another offer. He owned two buildings across the street. If we were interested, he would remodel the two into one building with a two bedroom apartment behind. What an offer. Our little apartment was so small. Greg's bedroom was a closet and the kitchen was strictly a one person room.

After about three months, our new store was ready. Herb's Little Hardware was now a big store. The apartment was fantastic with hardwood floors, two big bedrooms, a spacious bathroom and a kitchen with loads of cabinets and counters. Business increased and we had a larger inventory. We added a nursery and storage shed on the adjoining lot.

When we moved into the larger store, we attracted more attention and thieves. Our best alarm was our little dog, Flash. When she came into our bedroom at night growling, we knew we had prowlers. One evening after we closed the store, Flash, walked over to the window in our apartment growling. This window led out to an empty lot and was covered with screen door protectors. I looked out and noticed that someone had moved a board that lay next to the window. What I did next was rather stupid. I went out the back door and peeked around the corner of the building. I saw a fellow kneeling below the window. He apparently was trying to remove the screen guards. I picked up a short two by four and started to crawl toward him on my hands and knees. That side of the building was in the shade from the street lights which gave me protection. I was within ten feet of him when he turned and saw me. Well, the expression on his face and the way he took off ended our little incident. I never thought that he might have a gun. About six months later Flash came into the bedroom growling. When I followed her, she immediately went to the door leading into the store. I peeked out into the store and could see nothing amiss. One of my customers had ordered a real good pistol. By the time it arrived, he had already found one at another store. I was going to send it back when Marnie said, "After that last attempt, why don't you keep it." This time I had a pistol in hand. After waiting a while and hearing nothing, I turned the lights on. At that moment, a horn sounded in back of the building. I could hear someone running across the lot. I went out into the store and found my front door lock completely jimmied. Thieves almost succeeded moving the very heavy bar from across the front double doors. When the police arrived the next day, Marnie and I were informed that we had been visited by the "Double Door Bandits" who had a very bad reputation for rape, robbery, and assault. We were lucky. Thanks to Flash.

Luck was with us in another incident during Christmas season. It was getting close to closing when this young fellow came into the store to cash a check. He was so close to the cash register that he was able to look into it before I could close it. He left and I did not pay any more attention to him. I had finished with the last customer and was going to close the door when this character returned with his hat pulled low, his coat collar up and his hand in his pocket. He came right up to me. All I could think was that I am going to lose my money and I better not argue. Luck was with me. That very minute, our friends, the Kennedys, arrived through the back door. Ilene Kennedy, who has a very loud and high voice, came through the store door. "Hi Herb." This would-be robber made a u-turn and headed out the door.

Our life was to improve again. A friend brought his 11 year old son, Ralph, to the store and asked us to put him to work. Ralph was an amazing young boy. He was not doing well in school; but he was a genius in our store. Everybody liked him. He was one terrific salesperson. He would one day own and operate the biggest hardware store in the bay area.

More hopes were filled when we found out that we would have another baby. It just had to be a girl. Marnie's mother, Melie, arrived to help out with the house. It was an exciting trip to the hospital. That changed to disappointment when the doctor arrived and said to me, "We sure don't need you around here. Why don't you go home?" The phone rang that night. It was a girl so that's how Barbara entered our family. Marnie and I decided that this would complete our family, one boy and one girl.

We were closing one day when a customer asked Marnie and me if we might be interested in joining the Oakland Rod and Gun Club. We both became very excited when we attended the first meeting. We had been rather socially exempt due to running the store seven days a week and having two babies. We met friends through this club and many of the friendships would last a lifetime. Marnie and I along with Ed and Edie May Dimond, Ralph and Helen Mays, and Lou and Julie Brooks had some wonderful times camping, hunting, and fishing together.

Ed eventually bought a duck club where our group spent a lot of time in the fall. Marnie and I were up at his club one year when he was remodeling the duck shack. The gals decided to go shopping. I had taken Marnie's billfold out of her purse and forgot to tell her. She came back and told Edie, "I'm going to give Herb the devil for taking my purse." Edie said, "Here. Take this rolling pin. He is out back on the ladder." I was coming up the ladder carrying a window when she reached out the window to wave the rolling pin at me. Well, that rolling pin and my head met at the same time. I almost fell off the ladder and Marnie thought she had killed me.

Our group decided to go deer hunting in Utah. The trip was great with lots of scenery. Our first night in Salt Lake City, we went to a restaurant that specialized in chicken. The waitress brought a dish with rolled up washrags because a lot of the eating was by hand. Never one to let humor pass by, Ed put one of the washrags on his plate and covered it with ketchup. He was pretending to be cutting it up and Ralph was wiping down his bald head with another washrag when the waitress returned with our coffee. The waitress could not believe what was happening.

We, guided by Ralph's brother Bob who is a native of Salt Lake City, finally made camp back in the hills. The next morning Ed said to Bob, "You got the coffee on yet?" "Oh did you not know you don't drink coffee when you are Mormon?" It was a whole week before we were able to buy some coffee.

Our hunting was not too great. We did take some does on a special hunt. On our way home, we went by the packing house to pick up our venison. We noticed a huge bunch of antlers behind the packing house. We asked the manger about taking some and he said, "Help yourself." We loaded the top of the truck with horns which was a big attraction on the way home. It is a wonder that the state cops did not stop us.

Our life was very comfortable for the next two years. We made some very nice trips leaving Ralph to run the store. He loved this extra responsibility. He always surprised us with special sales. The following year was to change. Discount houses moved into Oakland. We had no way to compete. That year our five-year lease would expire and Jack Kohn died of a heart attack. Mrs. Kohn, who thought that Jack had been giving us too good of a deal, doubled our rent. We could not afford to stay and the rent was too high to sell the business. Only one choice faced Marnie and I—close it up. My dad and mother joined us so Dad stayed and helped sell out the store. I went to work for Shuey and Diamond Dairy.

During the last two years of owning the store, brother George and I bought two lots at Lake Tahoe. We finally finished a small cabin on one of the lots. George was in the orange juice business. He decided to open a route to Lake Tahoe. He would take the route on Fridays and I would go on Tuesdays. The delivery took 24 hours round trip. Marnie and I would go to San Jose, where the juice company was located, at two o'clock in the morning to load the truck with juice. By morning we would be in Tahoe to start our deliveries around the lake. If we got rid of the load, we stayed over in the cabin. Otherwise we would have to return to San Jose. The orange juice business lasted through the summer. When fall came, the tourists quit Lake Tahoe. Therefore we lost the demand for orange juice.

Melie and A. J., Marnie's parents, were great help to us. A. J. was a great father-in-law. He loved California and the weather. Melie and A. J. had recently retired after running a restaurant in Parkston, South Dakota for forty-three years. We enjoyed their company many times while we had the store. With George and Phyllis living in San Jose and Vince and Kay living in the San Quin Valley, we had lots of get-togethers when Melie and A. J. visited.

Mom and Dad spent over three years with us. Dad enjoyed California. When we had the store, we used to go up into the gold country for firewood which we sold at the store. I remember one trip. It was in January and we had stopped in Stockton for some doughnuts. Making a stop along the side of the road to enjoy coffee and these doughnuts, Dad was looking over a very green pasture full of white-faced cattle. He said, "You know they told me back in South Dakota that January was like this. I did not believe them."

One other trip we were returning with a load of wood when we spotted a tomato field full of ripe tomatoes. I stopped and asked a field hand if it would be possible to pick some. "Help yourself. The cannery is through and we are going to disk them up tomorrow." There must have been a hundred acres of tomatoes. Marnie and I were going up and down the rows picking the big ones when Dad who was behind us said, "Hey, young lady. You missed one."

Marnie loved to tease Dad. When we were living behind the store and knowing that Dad and I were in the store, she called on the phone and asked for Mr. Johnson. When Dad answered she said, "This is Montgomery Wards and I am calling about your overdue bill." "Yes ma'am. I will tell the Mrs." Poor Dad was rather shook up because he always paid his bills. After a pause, Marnie said, "Now you come on back for coffee." Years later while we were visiting back in South Dakota, an old timer told me that Dad paid back his seed and feed loan during the depression. He said, "Hell, no one paid those bills back."

Marnie and I were very active in East Bay Veterans of Foreign Wars. One year we attended the convention at San Diego. We stopped at Andersons Split Pea Soup Restaurant. While visiting with a fellow at the adjoining table, he informed us that he lived in Roseburg, Oregon. We mentioned that we were considering moving out of the bay area. "Why don't you come up to Roseburg, Oregon and look at my town." We decided right then to take him up on his offer.

Now, back to the convention in San Diego. It turned out to be a real wild time. We had just checked into the hotel and gone down to the hospitality room by the pool. One of the wives of a delegate was a little inebriated and jumped into the pool with all her clothes on. The manager informed her that she could not be in the pool with her clothes on so she quickly removed them. That night, another delegate hired a brass band. At two in the morning he took them down all the halls in the hotel while they played marching songs. What a night! These were the good old days for conventions. The police were great. Any delegate that was getting too far out downtown was only loaded in the squad car and hauled back to the hotel. I was commander for our post for two years. At the end of my term, they presented me with a lifetime membership in the VTW. Our post or ship was a great bunch. Marnie was president of the auxiliary.

After closing the hardware store, we had to decide where we were going to live and what I would look for in the job line. Jim Hutchinson an old customer of the store came up with the answer. "Come down to Shuey Diamond Dairy and drive a milk truck for a while." It was a good job. For the first time in a few years, I had no worries. I just had to drive the truck and deliver the milk. It was a different view of the public. I found out that being a milkman was not too bad of a position. Some of the customers could not be nice enough. Only a few were snobs. It was the nickel and dime aristocrats that were the big trouble. The real wealthy were fantastic. Mrs. Lerner, who owned the dress shops, always had a piece of cake and coffee at every delivery. Mr. Flair of Catapillar Company always wanted to have a coffee visit. He owned 45 acres in the middle of Piedmont.

I had been driving for about a year when the supervisor called me into his office. "Johnson, we need another swing driver. As you know quite a few of the routes, why don't you take the job? You have to know all the routes as a swing driver. It does have a few advantages which include extra pay and time off." When I told him O.K., he said Swanson would break me in. The following day, Swanson showed me the routes. We were in the black district of Richmond when he told me to take two quarts of milk across the street to an apartment building. He said, "Be sure to collect for the milk." I rang the door bell and a very attractive colored girl came to the door in a very short robe. I held the two quarts toward her and said, "I have to collect." What happened next threw me for a real loss of composure. She let her robe open and stepped toward me. I was holding two quarts of milk between two very noticeable boobies. I do remember her saying, "Mr. Milkman, we do not pay for our milk in cash." I headed for the truck where Swanson was having a laughter fit.

As a milk truck driver, I was responsible for any shortages in the day's balance. On pay day, the shortages were totaled and deducted from my paycheck. Any overages were not credited. One day as I was checking out my load, I noticed they had given me a case of quarts of whipping cream in place of skim milk. Out on the route, I called Marnie to meet me and I sent her home with 12 quarts of whipping cream. The neighborhood had a real treat.

Driving a milk truck was supposed to be a temporary deal for me. I was out on the route when I made up my mind this was enough of this life for me. I turned the truck and went back to the plant where I told the supervisor that I was quitting. "I will put your two week notice in." "No way. I'm quitting right now." The move turned out to be right. I had already met Mr. Lycette who owned a lot of property and was looking for a person to work between him and the managers.

It was this same year that Marnie and I found a home in East Oakland that just suited our expectations. Two bedrooms with a shop and garage that had a small apartment in the rear area. Between the two of us, we came up with a plan to attach the garage to the house with a utility room. This would give us three bedrooms, two baths, a utility room, and a very large family room. I went to the building department with our plan only to be turned down. You will only end up with a rental and this is a one family area." Marnie and I don't know the meaning of the word "quit." In the next two years, we completed our plan. We even re-sided the house with a brick veneer at the base of the siding.

It was during this time that Marnie and I met Pat and Frank Latimore. Frank worked for U. S. Plywood. He asked me one day if I was interested in hard wood. "We receive plywood panels from the Philippines cased on hardwood crates. Some of it's ash and several kinds of mahogany." It did not take me long to say yes because I had a shop and loved working with wood. He said, "Anytime I get a pallet full of this crating, I will call you to pick it up." I was surprised with the first load. There were mahogany rough boards nine foot long and eight to twelve inches wide. It was just beautiful lumber for free. I asked the high school if I could use their shop sizer and received an O. K. In no time, I had a real supply of finished mahogany and ash. Then came gun cabinets, shelves, etc. I even sided the house with board and lap mahogany. When we sold the house, the new owner said, "I know I am probably wrong. That siding sure looks like furniture wood." I built a hutch out of mountain ash and left one door with rough wood inside including the printing from the shipper just as a gag to prove where the wood came from. Marnie and I had many good times with Pat and Frank. It was with deep sadness when he informed us that he had an incurable form of leukemia.

Our dreams of having a little wet bar began when we owned the little hardware store. Before we moved across the street to larger quarters, the old building was occupied by an attractive red headed woman who made commercial signs. I was over talking to her one day about a sign for our little hardware store when she told me that the kind of signs she produced were very expensive because the process involved sandblasting. I was leaving when she asked, "Would you care for a free one? I have one here that the business went broke before it opened due to a divorce." It was a mirror about two foot high and four foot long. On the mirror was a partially clad lady sandblasted and painted, and the names Lydia and Johnny. I could not resist it, even with no place to store it. I took it home and told Marnie, "Someday we will build a bar around this."

Our home had one problem. Our driveway, which was about 50 feet long, had a crack running down the length. It continually kept shifting. One month it would widen and the next close up. Sometimes, one edge would be about an inch above the other. I kept putting in sand and cement, and wet it down with the hope it would stay put. Ernie, my neighbor across the street, was adding on to his house and had poured the footing for the addition. He came over one morning. "Herb, come over here and look at my footing." Right through both sides was a large crack. We were discussing his problem when I happened to look across at my driveway. My cracked driveway and his crack were in perfect alignment. I called the university. What should you guess? I had been trying to patch the Hayward Fault. They informed me that the fault had not been active for many years.

Working with Mr. Lycette was very interesting. He had a lot of apartments that needed repairing. What I did not want to do was supervise the repairs. I guess I saved him quite a bit of money. He told me one time, "Herb, anytime you even think about my business, even if you are in bed, you charge me. He called me one night about twelve. He asked me to meet him at Chuck Cauglans Restaurant. He had a big paddock and hasp which he had me install on the front door with papers. Chuck was in arrears with his rent.

After four days, I met Earl again. He walked over to the bar and picked up two quarts of whiskey. He said to me, "Take the rest. What you don't take, you haul to the dump." Here was a big restaurant full of foods of all kinds, even a big prime rib roast in the cooler. I had a pickup full of booze, another of food from frozen prawns and a thirty gallon can of flour. When it came to the ice cream cabinet, there were about ten three gallon cans. Some were half full and others full. I had no way of storing them and was planning on taking them to the dump. While loading them on the truck, a fellow approached me and inquired about what I was doing with all the ice cream. I said, "I am going to the dump if they are still here when I get back. I will be gone about half an hour." Well when I came back, the ice cream was gone.

All of these supplies came in real handy. We partied and partied. We had finished the big family room with a complete wet bar. You asked for a certain drink, we had the makings. Marnie and I found this real good jute box and piano for our family room. One night, the jute box quit so we called for service. The fellow who came said, "I don't remember being in this bar before."

# CHAPTER 8

## The RV Years

## 1962—1990

Our love of RV traveling really came about through a business venture. My brother George, who was in the orange juice business, dropped by one day. "Herb, how would you and Marnie like to get in on a little side business." With the hardware store, we really did not need more investments. Yet, the old adventure spirit took over and we could not say no. The business was an orange juice route to Lake Tahoe. It looked like everything would work out because we had help for the store on the day we needed to take the route. It started in San Jose and then went on to Lake Tahoe which George said would probably be a twenty-four hour trip up and back. We had a cabin at Tahoe that would give us a place to stay.

The first step was purchasing a one ton truck and building a covered box on it. With everything completed, George and I loaded the truck with orange juice and headed for the lake. The stores and restaurants at Tahoe gave us a good reception. We left the lake and headed for San Jose with an empty truck. The route called for two deliveries a week. Marnie and I took Friday and George took Monday. We did not have a permit to cross the line into Nevada. Therefore, the managers from the casino met us on the California side and picked up their orange juice.

Marnie and I left home at twelve at night to go to San Jose and load the truck by two o'clock so we could reach Tahoe by daylight. By the way, baby Gregory accompanied us. One night while we were loading, Marnie looked in the cab where Gregory was sleeping. What a shock. There was no baby! We went out the front loading door to find Gregory holding his blanket and watching a freight train go by.

The weather at the lake controlled our sales to a certain extent. One trip after it had been cold for a week, we found the stores still well stocked. If we could not get rid of all our juice, it meant going back to San Jose for cold storage. We parked on the west side of the lake for lunch. Gregory was sucking on a bottle of juice as usual when this little boy came over. "Where did your boy get the orange juice?" "We have a whole truck load." The boy's mother came over and asked, "Would you sell me a couple of quarts?" We stayed right there and unloaded our entire stock. That night we stayed at our cabin and did a little gambling.

When the season ended, we decided to keep the truck to use for our store. It was also very handy for camping out. I made a bed in the front of the box. With a Coleman stove and lantern, we enjoyed many outings. Greg slept in the bed while Marnie and I made up a bed on the floor. I remember one night at the Oregon Creek campgrounds. Greg was asleep and Marnie and I watched the stars with our heads on the tailgate. How romantic! The truck stayed with us after we left the store. We finally sold it when we moved to Delmont Street in Oakland.

Marnie and I were out for a Sunday afternoon drive when she suddenly said, "Turn around and go back. I just saw something in a driveway back there." There sat a beautiful red pickup with a red camper mounted on it. The camper was an eight foot over the cab style. To our amazement, a "For Sale" sign was on the windshield. We knocked on the door to ask the price and if we could look inside. The little camper had everything with stove, ice box, table, lots of cabinets, a bed over the cab, and an additional bed that could be made up from the dinette set. The price was four thousand dollars.

We hashed over finances and payments that night. The next day we called the owners and said we would take it. We were so excited that we never even tried to talk the price down. The camper fit our travel plans perfectly. Barb and Greg rode in the back while we traveled. The beds were just right. Marnie and I slept over the cab while Greg and Barb slept in the breakfast unit.

Our first trip was for opening of the trout season at Calveras. There were always five or more couples who went on this outing. The first afternoon was spent setting up tents. Marnie and I pulled up in our camper, found a level spot, put out our camp chairs, and mixed a drink. What a hullabaloo we heard from the rest of the couples.

We decided to drive back to South Dakota and visit the folks. When we arrived at Marnie's mother's place in Parkston, Melie took one look at our new camper and asked me to park it in the alley. All the neighbors came over to see our little jewel. They even asked us to drive it in the Centennial parade. Melie said to Marnie, "Why didn't you buy a nice car like your sister Phyllis?" All the attention the local people showed helped Melie decide we could park the camper in her driveway.

On one trip, we were looking for cherries at fruit stands. I slowed down almost to a stop at one fruit stand and then pulled back onto the highway when I saw they had no cherries. Barb and her cousin Dave were in the back as usual. Dave started pounding on the back of the camper. Barb had jumped out thinking we were going to stop. I looked in the rear view mirror and saw her running down the highway waving her arms. Poor little girl. She was in tears fearing we were leaving her.

Although we had some very good times in our many trips taken with that little camper, more room for the four of us was needed. Brother Leonard called from Sacramento to tell us he was now a Ford truck salesman and that Ford had just come out with a Campers' Special Pickup. It was a larger and roomier truck than our current truck. Our camper and truck sold quickly after I put an ad in the paper so we boarded the train for Sacramento. We had not decided whether to buy a trailer or a larger camper. We had a four wheel trailer for moving which this new Ford truck could handle perfectly.

After moving up to Oregon, our next recreation vehicle was a sixteen foot trailer. This unit did not fit with our plans. Maybe this was because we were used to having a compact camper. After a few trips with this trailer, we took off for a camper dealer in Eugene. We purchased an eleven foot over the cab camper. Our family kept this unit for two years until motor homes started getting popular. That's when an ad in our daily paper changed our mode of transportation. We found a twenty foot Winebago motor home for eighty-five hundred dollars. It was a little old, 1973, but had only twenty thousand miles. Our trailer went up for sale and we became motor home owners.

Two years later after many pleasant trips in the motor home, we had an extra large apple crop. Marnie and I loaded the pickup with apples and headed out on a peddling route. That afternoon with just two boxes of apples left, we traveled to Junction City which is the home of many RV dealers. Passing this one RV lot, we spied this thirty foot Southwind motor home. "Let's pretend to look at the motor home and see if we can get rid of the last two boxes." Well, we did, but in the sales process, we ended up with the Southwind. Oh, we did get twelve thousand dollars trade-in for the Winebago. That left a balance of eighteen thousand dollars.

We now had lots of room with a full bath, a big bedroom with a divan that could be made into a bed, and a pull down bed above the driver's seat. The breakfast unit also made up into a bed. There was room to sleep eight. Wrong. Marnie and I invited three other couples to go to the Octoberfest at Mount Angel. It was a perfect day and we all enjoyed the Bratwurst and cabbage dinner. Well that night after we finally all bedded down, it was a gas attack. There is just not enough space for eight people with this condition.

When Marnie retired, we decided to take an extended trip around the United States. Herman and Cleo Plouff (very close and old time friends) asked if they might travel with us. They pulled a thirty-two foot trailer with a Suburban. We were very pleased for the company. We decided to travel by secondary roads and stay off the freeway as much as possible. This decision turned out to be perfect with lower gas prices, food stands and opportunity to get closer to the local people. All the little towns we wandered through were great.

Leaving Seattle, we drove east on Highway 2 all the way to Michigan. Our first major attraction was playing golf outside Glacier National Park and then visiting the park. What beautiful scenery. We then went across Idaho with all its beautiful mountains and lakes. We picked and ate field corn in North Dakota. Bears came into the campground in Minnesota. A storm caught us while we were crossing the Maginaw Bridge in Michigan. Herman had to take his shoestrings out to tie up my awning. The awning was rolled up but the wind was so strong that it still unwrapped it. We spent the night at a Catholic Church parking lot with the blessing of the father. We had the awning repaired the next day.

Our next stop was to visit my old ship mate, Bob Doyle, and his wife Dottie. I stood up for them when they were married in New Orleans. What a visit we had. We even speared salmon at his hunting lodge. We left there with our freezer full of salmon. Herman's mother, uncles, and son Greg live close to Detroit. We parked right in Greg's yard and enjoyed a week of visiting and dining. Leaving Detroit, we headed for Niagara Falls. What a site! It was a beautiful day. We even went through the tunnel behind the falls.

New York and the Statue of Liberty was our next destination. While going through New Jersey right in a downtown area, the strap that held the pull down bed broke. Marnie and I drove through the business district with the bed sitting on our heads until we found a place where we could turn off. We visited the old railway station where all the immigrants took their trains. It had gates for fourteen trains and was in the process of restoration. After visiting the Statue of Liberty, we spent the night in the parking lot. I went out after dark. It was raining, but there was that great lady all lit up.

We headed south down the coast and stopped at every public fishing dock and doughnut shop. Our camp sites varied from shopping malls to roadside rest stops. One afternoon, we decided to look up a campground. It was a very nice place right by a lake. I went over to inquire about an out of state fishing license. The lady in the office said, "You don't need a license here because we own the lake. But watch for alligators."

After shopping at a doughnut shop one morning, we came out to find pamphlets on our windshield. We were invited to spend four nights at an RV resort park near Kennedy Space Center. In the four days, we visited the center and all other nearby sites. The launch pad and rocket center were very overwhelming. Our last day, we went to a sales meeting to see if they could sell us a share in the park. It was a definite "No." It was unbelievable. They gave Herman and Cleo a microwave oven while Marnie and I chose a $100 savings bond for our gift. What a stop.

Miami and Key West were next. We even had to outrun a hurricane on the west side of Florida. We went on through Alabama and Mississippi to New Orleans. I looked up my old home from when I was in the navy. Forty-five years later, it looked the same.

Leaving New Orleans, we headed for Galveston. Bob Hall Public Fishing Pier was our major stop. Marnie and I went out on the pier at sundown. We had not caught anything when Marnie said, "I think I will walk out toward the end to see if anyone else is doing very well." She came back with this salt water cat fish weighing about two pounds. "A fellow out there gave it to me. Said Texans called them tourist trout." "Well let's clean it and give it a try." About this time, another fellow came by and said you two need more bait. You can have these two. We took the three back to the motor home so no one would see us and cleaned them. They were delicious.

After leaving here, we visited San Antonio with the Alamo and the canals. We also visited President Johnson's old home place. We then headed up to Granbury, Texas to visit my sister Lorraine and her husband, Ivan. We spent a month with them including Thanksgiving. One friend of Lorraine's loaned us his new bass boat. Another loaned us his extra car, a new Buick. The last two weeks, my sister Dolores and her hubby, Alfred, arrived so I had a companion on the fishing trips. We had good luck catching catfish. We put the surplus in Ivan's goldfish pond. Anytime we needed a catfish, it was just a matter of getting the net out and snaring one. This was a very good plan until we discovered that catfish love goldfish.

Ivan and Lorraine really entertained us with the best places for catfish and hush puppies. One night, they took us to a place that had been opened to the public until the state closed them down for having only one coed bathroom. We had the place to ourselves and had a big order in for catfish and hush puppies. After dinner which was terrific, the owners' two girls, turned on the juke box and taught us the Texas two-step. Lorraine's little dog had a time too—chasing mice across the dance floor.

Saying good-bye to Lorraine and Ivan, we headed for Arizona. Our stay in Arizona lasted only two weeks as we were getting homesick. We had been gone for seven weeks and traveled over eleven thousand miles.

While still owning the Southwind motor home, we found an 18 foot boat that we purchased. We made many fishing trips with it in tow. On a trip to Kootenay Lake in British Columbia, we met my cousins, Clayton and Elva Johnson. We had a grand time exploring the lake by boat and catching some nice fish.

Another fishing trip that Marnie and I will never forget was on the coast in Brookings, Oregon. It was bad from the start. We decided to take a different route after I suggested, "Let's go by way of Glendale and then take a road west to the coast." Arriving in Glendale which is about thirty miles from Roseburg, we inquired at a tavern about the route to the coast. "Just take Dollar Road right here at the edge of town," the fellow replied. It was about four in the afternoon when we started down Dollar Road. We met a pickup with two fellows in it as it was getting dark. I asked them, "Is this Dollar Road?" "No. Go back two miles to the bridge, cross it, take a left, and that will be your road." We did cross the bridge and took a left. After miles, our black topped road turned into a dirt road and then headed up the hills. At two in the morning, we found a sign that said Camas Valley twelve miles. We were just twenty miles from home with a motor home and trailer covered with dust.

We spent the night beside the road. With better expectations, we headed for Brookings to see our friends Ray and Carol Lockman. Had we known our little lark with destiny was not over, we might have turned around and gone back home. We arrived in Brookings where Ray and Carol and their friends, Milt and Philys, would be joining us for the fishing trip. That evening we decided to party at the Elks Club. It was two in the morning when we headed back to camp. I did not realize what a die hard fisherman Milt was until five o'clock that morning when I heard someone hammering on our motor home door. "Let's go fishing." While I got dressed, Milt and Ray hooked the the boat trailer to the motor home. We arrived at the ramp and

I backed the trailer down into the water. Ray hollered, "Boat's unhooked so go ahead." As I pulled up, I looked back in the mirror just in time to see both trailer and boat go into the water. Milt and Ray had forgotten to lock the hitch on the trailer.

I had safety chains installed the week before in Roseburg. Upon examination, we discovered the welder had only tacked the plates to the bumper and had forgotten to weld them. There we were ready to go fishing with our trailer at the bottom of the bay. I walked out on the dock where a fellow was fishing and he said, "I saw your trailer down there and it was still moving toward deeper water." I drove uptown to see if it was possible to find a diver and a vehicle with a winch. At that time of day there was no chance so I returned to the launch ramp. The lady in charge had called the Coast Guard and they had arrived. One of them was out on the dock casting a cable in the water with the hope of hooking the trailer. I said, "Let me try that. I don't think you are casting out far enough." A miracle happened. On the first cast out, I hooked onto something that was twenty feet out and forty feet down. I motioned for the fellow in the jeep to take up the cable and out came my trailer with the cable hook fastened to the dolly handle. What luck! I don't remember catching any fish. Yet it turned out to be a day to remember.

Marnie and Herb with their RV

# CHAPTER 9

## Roseburg and Family

## 1960—1970

Greg and Barb have been a great pleasure. Greg loves the outdoors for hiking, rock hunting, the heavens, and all of nature. Barb's tastes are different for sports and all the excitement of life. They both have enjoyed our campouts and I cannot remember a time when they were bored. We started our outdoor trips with the Ford one ton that we used to deliver orange juice to Tahoe. It had an enclosed box on the back which we used as a camper. We took many a trip we took with the truck to the mountains. Barb and Greg usually rode in the back. I had installed a hose with a funnel on each end for communicating. We were coming back from Tahoe one night when Greg hollered through the hose that he had to go to the bathroom. I found a spot to turn off and went back to help him out of the truck as it was gated. Well I ran into a stream as he was peeing over the tailgate.

Barb was always Dad's helper. I was repairing the roof on the storage shed one day when Barb climbed up to see what I was doing. It had not been over five minutes when I turned to see she was not on the roof anymore. I looked over the back of the roof and found she had fallen off into a blackberry thicket. I had to go down and fish her out of the brambles. She did not even have a scratch on her.

Greg was eleven years old when he went to work for Marnie's brother Vince. Vince and his brother-in-law, Kenny, owned forty head of Shetland ponies. They ran a riding concession at the city park during the summer months. Greg loved the ponies and became very good at handling them. His favorite pony was Pete, who always shared Greg's lunch, even tuna sandwiches. Greg gained lots of experience handling ponies and kids. One day when I helped load the kids on the ponies, I noticed Greg had a funny look on his face. All the kids had to be fastened with a safety belt. The girl Greg just loaded was a little hefty and the belt would not reach around her. Keeping the ring clean was another job. I saw Greg take off in a hurry with the scoop and shovel. He caught up with the pony and it all went into the shovel. These ponies were a great experience for both Greg and Barb.

While living in Delmont, our last place of residence in California, our life was very enjoyable. The kids had a lot of friends and our neighbors were great. We had finished the house and had been taking lots of trips. We were also very active in Oakland Rod and Gun Club. In the summer, it was off to the mountains for trout fishing. In the fall, it was up to Williams for duck hunting. I spent some time in the fall hunting deer. Unfortunately, my first West Coast kill was not until I was in Oregon. Our closest friends were from the gun club. Today I cannot help but pause and think of our group. Ed, Ralph, Lou, and Edie Mae are all gone. That is what happens when you approach eighty.

Oakland was changing. Greg came home from school telling us about problems at school. Kids were carrying knives and pipes in their socks. I was afraid for Marnie's work because she came home late at night. The paper was full of crimes. We had taken a few vacations to Oregon and remembered the fellow from Roseburg who told us to come up and see his town.

During Thanksgiving vacation we decided to take a trip to Roseburg. The town was a little smaller than we had expected. After looking around, we went to Mr. Lachey's real estate office. He sent us out with one of his salesmen. It was quite an experience. His car was not working and he asked if we could possibly use our camper. We found a house that we liked and told our aggressive salesman that we would think about it. It was lunch time and since he made no move to buy lunch, it was up to Marnie to cook lunch in our camper.

Marnie and I really liked the house. We thought we had better go to Eugene which was a larger city and look there before we decided for sure. We drove to Eugene that afternoon. After seeing a few houses, Barb said, "I don't like this town and want to go back to that house in Roseburg." Our feelings were mutual so we went back to Lackey's office the next day and gave them a down payment. Mr. Lackey told us that he would notify the people that lived there to move.

Back to Oakland. We put our two houses up for sale, including the Tahoe property. The same night that our ad for Tahoe came out, our good friends Julie and Lou Brooks called. "Didn't you know that if you ever sold your Tahoe cabins, we wanted to buy them?" Well, that closed the Tahoe property. Within a few months, our houses also sold.

I had built a large trailer and with our new Ford pickup. We decided to move ourselves. It was spring in Oregon so the weather was nice. When we arrived with our first load, we found that the people were still in the house. What a fast move they made leaving the house in a mess. Our new house was located about two miles from town. A school bus picked up Greg and Barb. The neighbors seemed nice and I started job hunting.

Life was a bit slower after living in the big city. Marnie joined the "New Comers" through which we met a lot of people. I transferred my VFW membership to the one in Roseburg. The commander was a retired preacher who informed me that no alcoholic beverages would be allowed. What a change after all the good VFW parties we had enjoyed. One meeting, he informed the group that the District Commander was attending our next meeting. I volunteered to barbeque chicken. He wanted to know if I could have mashed potatoes and gravy which I convinced him was not a proper menu. At that meeting, I was out in the side yard barbequing chicken and it was extremely hot. A lady came over and asked me if I would enjoy a cold beer. As I found out she was the District Commander's wife, I accepted. I saw our commander peeking out the door. The following meeting I was raked over the coals. Well that ended my interest in the local VFW.

The main attraction in Roseburg was its annual rodeo. Marnie, Greg, Barb, and I arrived an hour early the first time we went. Being used to the crowds in the Bay Area, we wanted to be sure of obtaining a good seat. Well, we had the whole place to ourselves for the hour. The rodeo finally started with the calf dressing for the first event. A horseback rider would rope a calf weighing in at about two hundred and fifty pounds. He would leave the calf on about fifty foot of rope and it was up to two teenagers, usually girls, to catch the calf and put a pair of pants on its hindquarters. It's a lot of excitement to see two girls get knocked down trying to catch a 200 pound calf. Barb made up her mind that that was her project for the coming year. That winter, I bought a calf, brockel faced, for her to practice on. She invited our neighbor girl to be her partner. By spring, that poor calf wore pants most of the time.

Spring and the day of the rodeo arrived. The two girls signed up for the calf event to find out they were the smallest and youngest pair in the event. I was working on Highway 5 about forty miles from home the next day. At lunch break one of the fellows said, "I saw the damnedest thing at the rodeo yesterday. Two little girls took the calf dressing event. They beat out girls who were way older." I guess you know what my next words were. "That was my daughter and her friend."

Employment was a problem in the Roseburg area. The economy was very poor. I applied at a mill. After I filled out the application, the personnel officer called me in. "Mr. Johnson, do you know what our wages are here?" "No." "Well, the starting pay is $2.10 an hour. Looking at your past record, I don't think you want to work here." That was my thought also. I finally found a job remodeling an office trailer for Houck Construction Company on highway 5. At that time, I inquired to the supervisor about the possibility of obtaining work with the construction crew on the highway once I completed the remodeling job. He replied, "Our flag man wants to quit. If you want the job, it's yours." The pay is $8.50 per hour." That was more than I was charging the company for my work!

Working on highway 5 was quite a change for me with big equipment and a different breed of men. The roar of so many engines all the time made it mandatory that you used hand signals. I started as flag man and was promoted to dump boss after three months. The pay was good. I was in charge of dumping the rock in the right places. There were fifteen belly dumps that did not stop while dumping. One is leaving while two are coming for eight hours a day. What a drag.

When we finished that section of highway 5, the crew moved on to a section in California. I did not want to move so the superintendent assigned me to a subsidiary, Beaver State Construction Company which was located in Roseburg. The economy in this area was very poor. Many of the lumber mills closed so work was hit and miss with Beaver State. I had been with them about a year when I decided to buy some equipment and go into business on my own. It was a lot of hard work; but it paid off. With Marnie working part time we were able to pay off the equipment and even take a few trips around the state.

Marnie and I had some money from the sale of property in California so we decided to buy some property here. One of our purchases was an old hotel and trailer park. We joined the two together and named it Shady Acres. It was not the best investment. Located in the poor part of town, it did not attract the best clientele. Most of the renters were on welfare. We would have to wait thirty days to get our rent. Sometimes the state would give the welfare recipient cash instead of a check made out to us. You guessed it. They would have a big party and then move out with no way for us to collect. We did have a few faithful tenants. One lady tenant paid us on time; but I noticed a lot of cars coming and going. She was in business on my property as a prostitute. I told her she would have to move. She said, "If I move, I might lose my welfare check." "Good-Bye Mrs. Brown."

Shady Acres meant lots of work and not much profit. It was not dull though. One time, Marnie and I were putting a little patch of grass in front of one of the units. We had just sat down for a breather when this fellow riding a motorcycle came in to visit a friend. We paid no attention to him until he left—right through our newly planted lawn. He hit the highway and then turned back to his friend. He had his back to me when I stomped up to him. "If you want that damn motorbike wrapped around your neck, just try that again." He turned around and stood up. Well he was taller than me, broader than me, and had a full beard. I was just about ready to run when he said, "No sir." I walked away like I had just whipped a bunch of wildcats.

Barb and Greg were very active in 4-H and used the extra space at Shady Acres for their sheep. Greg was very good at shearing sheep and won an award for his speed. Barb showed her lamb at the annual lamb show and also won an award. I rented thirty acres near where we lived on Kent Street so Greg could have more sheep. Later on, we started buying baby calves at the Live Stock Auction. Some we raised and some we buried. They were delicate little animals. Once they made it through the first month, the calves' survival chances were good. The sheep also had a problem—dogs. Marnie became very proficient with a shotgun. Marnie and I went to Eugene one day. When we arrived home, we found out Barb had dyed her pet lamb pink for Easter.

That same lamb had problems when it grew up. It was about to have its first lamb when I noticed things were not progressing right. Upon examination, I discovered the poor ewe was trying to give birth with the baby's front legs hanging back. I told Barb that the only way that ewe was to survive was to pull out those legs. Brave little Barb reached inside and pulled the legs forward. The baby lamb arrived O.K.

Brother Justin came to help me with my work. Soon after his arrival, Marnie and I found an old prune dryer on five acres with a large shed and a forty foot trailer. It was just the right place for my equipment and Justin. He really loved the place. He enjoyed inviting Marnie, the kids, and I over for Sunday Breakfast. He was a good cook. His neighbors, Tom and Elizabeth Hutton, had him over for many meals and to play cribbage with Tom.

I had to deliver five yards of shale to a customer on Woodward Creek. Justin asked to go along which turned out to be a true blessing. We had to cross a home-made bridge which I was very doubtful about. The owner of the bridge assured me that loaded ten yard trucks had crossed it. I had no reason to be skeptical. Justin got out of the truck to walk across the bridge first and to watch it as I came across with the truck. I was about half way across when I heard a loud crack and felt myself turning over. The truck and I went down twelve feet and landed upside down. At first I was knocked out. Then I heard Justin yelling, "Get out of the truck!" I was upside down still wearing my hard hat which was full of transmission grease. The truck's shift rod had popped out. I realized I was upside down. The window on the driver's side was crushed and it was impossible to get out. When I realized gas was leaking, I knew I had to move soon. Luckily the window on the passenger side was smashed out and it gave me an exit. The creek banks were too steep for Justin to get down to the truck to help me. After walking down the creek a ways I found a way out. Justin had already located help and the fire department was on its way.

Justin stayed with us for several years and drove dump truck for me. He was a good operator with the truck. Barb could have killed him when he showed up with the dump truck at junior high school to take her home. He always had a little trouble with checks that had no account. One Christmas, he bought us all very nice presents. Yes, he had charged them to Marnie and me. He borrowed our new van one night without asking and sideswiped a car. He got a ticket for hit and run. I went to court with him. The ticket was for five hundred dollars. The judge reduced it to one hundred fifty dollars. "Boy we were sure lucky," said Justin. In spite of all the problems, Justin was a good employee and made good money for Marnie and me. He was also a good brother. Justin wanted to get on the road again. As much as I hated to see him go, I knew from past experiences that when the wanderlust hit him, it was for the best to let him go.

The wanderlust spirit had been with Justin since the day he was able to get on his feet. Before the age of twelve, the spirit kept him not too far from home. At the age of twelve, he just said "Goodbye" and left. It was almost two years before the folks heard from him. He was down in Missouri working for an older couple who were very happy with him. When he finally returned home, it was just for a short time. Soon he was off again. Justin loved carnivals. Anytime one visited our town, he would leave with it. Dad and Mom were exasperated by his indifference. There were times he was picked up by the law for crimes such as petty theft and his favorite, writing checks with no money in the bank.

To my parents' dismay, Justin was drafted into the army. They just could not keep track of him. One time, to the embarrassment of the folks, the

MP's showed up at my folks' home looking for Justin. We found out he was finally found working in a coal mine in Idaho. Justin believed in sharing what he had and what you had. If he had anything that he thought you might want, there was no question. It was yours. In spite of all the problems, he received an honorable discharge from the army. Justin made many more friends than enemies. You could not criticize him in front of his nieces and nephews. They all loved him. I was always glad to see him show up.

Marnie and I were members of the Lions Club for several years. The social life was great in addition to helping the community with many projects. Several members, including us, always stopped at the local pub after the meetings. It was at one of these gatherings that one of the fellows said," Let's go together and open up a pub of our own." This started the ball rolling. A few weeks later, five families contributed five thousand dollars each to put the plans in place. These families included my son and daughter with their spouses. One of our members had an older two story home on a busy street that, with some remodeling, would make a good tavern.

Greg and I, with the help of the group, took over the remodeling job. We had hopes of finishing the job with the money on hand; but it ended with a loan from the bank for an additional twenty thousand dollars. The city had stepped in with a lot of extras that we had not planned for.

Our tavern became the Vintage and Brew. At the grand opening, everything seemed to be a complete success. We had a light restaurant upstairs with pool and games downstairs. We had a small stage complete with a piano and PA system upstairs that we used to entice anyone with talent to perform. We had a lot of takers. Saturday nights a mixture of everything from old time hoe downs to solo entertainers. Marnie and I loved to take over on Friday and Saturday nights because of the entertainment.

The tavern business kept growing. Our group decided to sell when the beer business reached one hundred kegs per month. Sale price of taverns was gauged at one thousand dollars per keg per month. The beer business reached 95 kegs per month when the recession hit Roseburg. Business dropped and we found ourselves short of money to pay rent and help. The group decided to sell out at a loss. We each lost our initial investment. It was quite an experience for Marnie and I with the loss; but we still have good memories of the tavern.

After raising calves, I decided to graduate to cattle. I had a friend, Don, who wanted to go into partnership with me. We found some pasture land, went to the auction, and bought a few head of cattle. Don's wife, Pat, wanted to have a pair for her own. Don told me to take her out to the auction and find a pair for her. "Herb, you know more about cattle than I so you take her." Well Pat picked out an Angus cow with calf. They were right off the range and were not used to being around humans. Pat wanted them anyway and assured me that they could be tamed down. I had the auction house deliver the pair to a corral of a friend. The following day Don called and said he was going to move the pair to the pasture. "Don, be careful. That old cow is pretty protective of that calf." "Herb, no problem. I will just grab the calf, run up the shoot into the trailer, and then climb over the side when the cow comes after me." Well it worked as planned. The only exception is that the cow chased Don into the trailer and also went through the trailer after Don. That was one mean cow. We never did tame her down. We did raise a very good calf though.

Don and I were looking for more pasture land when we saw an ad in the paper for eighty acres of land costing seventeen thousand. It was up in the hills. We drove up a very windy road and came to a tumbled down gate. Good Lord. This was just what I had been looking for since coming to Oregon. I wanted this for Marnie and I. Don looked around and said, "Herb, I don't like this place." When we got back home, Marnie and I went back so she could see the place also. That night we called the lady who ran the ad and offered a down payment. That was the beginning of Rancho La Vista.

# Our Family

Back row:  Joseph Tuma (Barb's son), Joe Tuma (Barb's husband), Matt (Greg's son), Greg (son), Bryan (Greg's son)

Middle row:  Michelle (Barb's daughter), Barbara (daughter), Carol (Greg's wife), Nathan (Greg's son)

Front row:  Dad and Mom

# CHAPTER 10

## Our Paradise

## 1970—2001

The house on Kent was put up for sale and we started our plans to eventually move up on the hill. The house sold very quickly so we moved out to Justin's place. Our new home was the old prune dryer. Our new land had been occupied many times over the years. In looking over the records at the court house, we found out it had been homesteaded in 1850 by a man named Zook. In the following years, the acreage had been sold many times; but never divided. Mr. Zook planted the first orchard of apple trees. Marnie and I spent many days on the hill planning where the house would be and cleaning the brush away from the apple trees. To our surprise, we found out we also had grapes and three varieties of cherry trees. The grape vines had taken to the trees over the years so you needed a ladder to pick grapes. We found the remains of three homes that had been built on this land. All were decaying to some degree and impossible to repair. We were also happy to find a spring that had been developed. The land had lots of second growth timber. The road into the land followed a ridge with some places very narrow and steep. It was a half mile from the main road to our land. Marnie, Greg, Barb, and I were all excited about establishing our home and decided on the name, Rancho La Vista.

My work in excavation and construction was going well. All my spare time was spent on La Vista and getting ready to move. I was so fortunate that Marnie was as excited about it since she was definitely not a rural person. Her young life had always been spent living in a small town. Here, we were going to establish a home in more or less wilderness. We had to develop our own water system, bring in an electric line and bring in a phone line. This was to say nothing about trying to improve a "trail" into a "road." The hill was beautiful with lots of big trees to protect us from the wind. There was a view everywhere you looked. We saw lots of deer, birds, and squirrels. In the spring, wild iris bloomed along our road.

Marnie wanted us to buy a mobile home rather than spend all the time it would take to build. We found the mobile home to suit us in Roseburg. Next came the excavation for the site which was right down my alley. The power company came through right on time. So did the telephone company. I put in the septic system. The day arrived for delivery of the home. It took a cat in front of the delivery truck and I ahead with the backhoe to clear out any trees or rocks along the half mile road into La Vista. The home came in two sections that were twelve foot wide and sixty foot long. After a lot of clearing and sweat, we finally had the sections in place. It took over a week to put the home together. What a great day it was when we no longer had to take a walk in the woods with a shovel. Instead, we had a bathroom.

The spring furnished water to take care of water needs except for the washing machine. Our next step was to drill a well. I had a dowser to decide where to drill. The spot he picked after much roaming with his copper rod was where two veins crossed only seventy-five feet down. The well driller went to work and at seventy-five feet had a dry hole. I told him to go ahead and drill deeper. We struck water at one hundred and fifty feet. Water was to be a problem on the hill. Over the years, we would have the well drilled several times before we hit a good well.

I was coming home from work one day when I found a young fellow examining some rocks along the ridge just outside our gate. When I asked him what he was looking for, he said, "Fossils." I asked him, "Why do the ridge to my left and the one to my right both have shale which I can use for road repair and this one has only sandstone?" His reply was, "This is a completely different formation. There is only one like this some thirty miles south. This ridge was formed from an up thrust in the earth's crust. I will tell you something else. It's still going up." I found out he was a geologist from the university.

Living on the ridge over the years, we realized that any earthquakes in the state could be felt here. Marnie and I were logging one day when she suddenly started waving for me to shut down the chain saw. "We just had an earthquake," she said. "I don't think so," I answered her. It was lunch time so we headed for the house. Marnie turned the water on and it was riel. I turned the television on and heard the news. San Francisco had just had a big quake. Our well had to be re-bored due to a cave-in.

Timber on La Vista was a real blessing. Any time Marnie and I needed some extra cash, we would get the chain saw and cat out. Marnie would run the winch on the cat and I would fall and buck. When we had a load or two ready, we would call for the self loader to haul them to the mill. I think the two of us made damn good loggers.

Life can change so fast and the unexpected can happen without warning. I faced death almost on a daily basis during the war years which was expected. Here in life away from conflict, a person takes life for granted. Marnie and I met Doris and Ray who are two people we really enjoyed and had a lot in common with. Ray and I fished and hunted together. Ray had a bad ankle from an injury while in the service so it was difficult for him to walk any distance. Rancho La Vista had a very good deer crossing by the front gate so I told Ray, "Just park your station wagon down by the gate and get your deer that way." He was very successful four years in a row. The last year, he parked there for several mornings and had no luck.

"Herb, if you see a buck, shoot it for me." I was just out of bed when I happened to look down at the gate. "Marnie, I guess Ray did not come up this morning. I don't see his station wagon." "Herb look! There is a buck coming up the road toward the house." I, still in my pajamas, grabbed my rifle and went out the door to try to get that buck. At that moment, a shot went off and down went the buck. Ray was parked out of sight behind an apple tree. He came up and told me the buck had come within fifteen feet of where he was sitting. He could not shoot though because of our buildings being there. As he started to bend over to dress the buck, he said, "Herb, I sure feel strange." I knew he had a bad heart so I told him, "Ray, you just go sit on the tailgate of your wagon and I will take care of the deer." All at once, I heard him say, "I have never felt like this," He fell over back into his wagon. I hollered at Marnie to call 911 and I started CPR. It was ten minutes before help arrived and it was too late for Ray. I have never felt so worn out before in my life as I did after that ten minutes of CPR. Yet it was to no avail. There lay my good friend Ray with a buck at his side. One of the rescue men said, "What a way to go." He may be right. We have a little cross that we keep decorated where Ray died.

Marnie and I celebrated our 25th wedding anniversary. At the time we were married, we had such a small wedding so we decided to go all out for our 25th anniversary. All of my family and most of Marnie's family attended. We held our party at the Floral Building at the fairgrounds. There were lots of food, a good band, and an open bar. Lorraine and Dick Malgren from California attended. They were our attendants at our wedding.

Greg finished high school and enrolled in Douglas Community College. He decided to put two years in and then attend Oregon State. While attending college, he met Carol. We were really pleased with her; but hoped for him to finish college before marriage. This was not to be. Love was to overcome our advice. They made a good couple, both attending college and working on the side to help pay expenses.

"For richer or poorer, in sickness and health." Those two believed in their vows for they experienced all. We almost lost Carol with a ruptured appendix. After many operations, she was told that she would not be able to have children. This was quite a blow. After graduation, Greg found a job in Sherman teaching agriculture.

Barb, in her last year of high school, signed up with a group of singers who toured Europe the following summer. What a time she had. Barb always leads an exciting life. She loved to travel and worked hard to pay for her adventures. Her love for music was to stay with her always. She also attended Douglas Community College. After college, she moved to Eugene with her pal Elaine. Barb held many positions from managing a credit union to managing a school cafeteria.

It was in Eugene where she met Joe Tuma. Joe was in the timber industry. Marnie and I gave them a very good wedding with many relatives from both sides attending. Barb made a beautiful bride and sang a love song, which she wrote for Joe.

All my family attended Barb and Joe's wedding so it was also to be the first Johnson reunion. These reunions would continue every other year, and would be in many parts of the United States and Canada. It was at the reunion held by the Peterson family that our first grandson, Bryan, would arrive. Greg and Carol had put in for adoption some months prior. It just happened that they were notified that a baby was available in Portland. What a reunion this was!

Joe worked many years in the lumber industry, including with International Paper, Bohemia and Willamette. His hard work moved him up from timber cruiser to log buyer. He is now in charge of logging crews. Joe is an excellent shopper. If there is a bargain, he will find it. He loves hunting and the outdoors.

In the years to follow, Joe and Barb blessed us with a baby girl, Michelle. Carol and Greg would be blessed with another boy, Mathew. It was an exciting day for them because they had just put in for another baby and expected to wait for a year or two. Joseph Jr. was the next arrival for Barb and Joe. Marnie and I now had four grandchildren. Several years would pass before any new addition. One day, Carol informed us that she was pregnant. This just could not happen with the report doctors had given her. Yet, it was so. Little Nathan arrived and was justly termed "Miracle Baby."

Michelle was born with a basketball in her hand. Through grade school and high school, she would become accomplished with basketball. She gave her parents and grandparents many proud moments following her games. Her accomplishment would award her a four year scholarship at Portland State University. Mathew also gave his parents and grandparents a great gift of pride with high school grades high enough to earn him the Ford Foundation Scholarship for four years at Oregon State. Bryan finished high school and moved to Bend, Oregon to attend community college. He worked part time jobs and also interned at a stock broker office. This experience gave him a chance to visit London where he visited the Merrill Lynch Stock Broker Office. Since returning home, he has taken a job with a banking firm. He also purchased a piano, has taken lessons, and has become very musical. His main love is fine clothes and cars.

My two youngest grandchildren, Joseph and Nathan, are proving themselves well. Joseph has a natural gift to make money. He started very young with a paper route and mowing lawns. I have never encountered another child who takes such good care of his toys and personal property. Joseph was denied sports in school due to injuries from a fall off the roof of his home that happened while he was helping his dad. He recovered after a long period. He is now in high school with good grades. I have no doubt this boy will succeed in life.

Nathan, in his young years, was not as tall as he would like to have been. He made up for it in speed. This put him on the team in soccer, basketball and especially football. He has given Marnie and I many happy times watching him play all his sports. Nathan is Grampa's right hand boy and at my beckoned call for every little job that I need help with. He is especially good at saying thanks and has lots of love.

Dad had a short fuse; but carried a lot of love in his heart. His love of little children was very deep, especially for his grandchildren. He loved the great outdoors, livestock, a good crop of corn, a chance to visit with friends, a game of horseshoe or pool, a cup of coffee with a biscuit, and most of all his family. I know he made mistakes such as moving too often with a large family. He was not the best at farming; but he left me with many solid traditions and memories. He was a great "Pop" as we often called him. Dad was born in 1897 and passed away in 1962 at the age of 75.

Mom stayed with us for eight more years. She enjoyed most of those years with her family and then in a retirement home. When I think of the years she spent out West, I can hardly understand how she survived. This included living in a two room shack with nine children, having to put out beds every night, and having a big galvanized tub as the only bathing equipment. Privacy was impossible. We heated with ignite coal which was not the best. She had to be doctor and nurse for any sickness or injury because the closest doctor was seventy-five miles away. She had a large health book which she consulted in emergencies. Feeding our large family was another challenge. Groceries were always in short supply. I remember seeing her grind government surplus cracked wheat in a coffee grinder so she could make muffins. Bread had to be baked every other day. When she had the right ingredients, she could make the best rolls and cakes. With all the washing clothes, cooking, and keeping the house clean, Mom still found time to teach us the songs and rhymes from her childhood. Her love was shared with us all. Mom was born in 1892 and left us in 1970 at the age of seventy-eight.

Starting as the fourth oldest in the family, I now find myself the oldest. Justin, who was never married, died in 1978 after a long illness. He rather misused himself traveling in the U.S. with carnivals which he dearly loved. George passed away in 1993 from cancer of prostate. He had parted from his wife, Phyllis, several years before. He had won the battle with alcohol. He left four very wonderful children, all grown up and settled in their professions. Howard died in 1996. He left his wife, Lillian, and three children. His children, one boy and two girls, are very well settled.

My brother, Bob (Robert), lives in Oregon with his second wife, Darlene. He parted from his first wife, Mary Lou, after fathering 13 children. He does a wonderful job of keeping in contact with his whole family. He is an invalid after losing a leg and having a stroke caused by an injury from World War II. Chuck (Charles) is terminal. He suffers from cancer of the prostrate. He leaves a wonderful family. Three children were born to him and his wife, Faith. Four additional children were adopted. It is a real pleasure to visit this family. Dolores lives close to us. She and her husband, Alfred, adopted a boy and a girl in their early years. They were unfortunate to lose their boy. They keep in close contact with their daughter in Montana. Dorothy and her husband, Butch (Raphael), live in South Dakota. They raised eight outstanding children, all good looking and very successful. Butch, Alfred and Mary Lou are Turbaks and married three Johnsons. Lorraine married Ivan Blachett and moved from South Dakota to Texas. They have three boys and two girls. Ivan passed away several years ago. Lorraine and her five are real Texans. Leonard, the youngest Johnson, lives in southern California. He recently lost his wife, Dorene. He has four boys.

It is with both sorrow and joy when death takes a family member. At these times, that the entire family joins together. Dad passed away after a long illness. The whole family gathered at Kranzburg, South Dakota. The reminiscing was great. Everyone had tales to tell about living with Dad. Alfred, my brother-in-law, told a story that was true to Dad's nature. In his last days while the minister was praying for him, Dad interrupted, "Just a minute Reverend. Somebody shut that grain off up there. That bin is full."

As I look back over the years, I realize how wonderful it is that Marnie and I have celebrated our fifty-second wedding anniversary, enjoyed two children, and adored five grandchildren. We have been so blessed. Thirty years have passed since our move onto Rancho La Vista. We more or less pioneered the hill with its eighty acres. Water had to be developed, electric lines brought in, and development of life sustaining items that so many people take for granted. We never stopped caring and noticing. La Vista brought us closer to nature. When Marnie and I looked up the past records of La Vista and read the many names of long gone residents who had each put effort into living here, it came so clear to me. We are all tenants of the Good Lord and each one gets their share of living on the land. You never really own anything.

I just enjoyed my eightieth birthday. I will never forget the night during World War II. Things were very rough that night. Japanese planes were coming in from everywhere. I knelt down by my twenty millimeter and asked the Good Lord, "Just let me live until I'm forty."

CPSIA information can be obtained
at www.ICGtesting.com
Printed in the USA
FSOW02n0151310815
10481FS